Growing Pains

Growing Pains

Navigating Teen Angst and Ortho Hurdles

Maria M

Mohammed Altaf Hussain

CONTENTS

Table of Content

Introduction

Understanding Teen Angst

Grasping High schooler Tension

The wild excursion from youthfulness to adulthood is set apart by a horde of personal disturbances, and at the very front of this tumult lies the bewildering domain of high schooler tension. Young people, on the cusp of self-revelation and freedom, wrestle with a perplexing embroidery of feelings, vulnerabilities, and personality emergencies that all in all structure the mosaic of their tension. This stage isn't simply a soul changing experience; it is an extraordinary period where hormonal vacillations, cultural assumptions, and individual yearnings unite to make a tempest inside the juvenile mind.

Developing Torments

High schooler apprehension is unpredictably woven into the texture of developing agonies, an inescapable piece of the formative interaction. As young people go through actual changes, hormonal floods, and the enlivening of their sexuality, the going with mental movements can appear as dissatisfaction, disarray, and a feeling of distance. The actual embodiment of developing torments lies in the discord between the developing self and cultural assumptions, leaving young people trapped in a sensitive dance among similarity and self-revelation.

The mission for independence frequently conflicts with the requirement for acknowledgment, making a favorable place for youngster tension. Peer connections become the overwhelming focus during this stage, with the longing to fit in and be figured out filling the profound disturbance. The battle to get comfortable with oneself and lay out an extraordinary personality turns into a combat zone where the setbacks are many times confidence and profound prosperity. As youngsters wrestle with the maze of cultural standards, familial assumptions, and individual desires, the clamor of clashing requests adds to the ensemble of their apprehension.

Exploring High schooler Apprehension and Ortho Obstacles

Understanding and exploring youngster tension require a nuanced approach that considers both the mental and physiological elements of youthfulness. Ortho obstacles, addressing the snags that ruin the smooth movement through immaturity, add an extra layer of intricacy to this all around unpredictable excursion.

One critical ortho obstacle is the instructive scene, where scholastic tensions and the quest for greatness can become overpowering. The progress from center school to secondary school increases scholarly assumptions, and teens frequently end up wrestling with the requests of thorough coursework, state administered testing, and the approaching phantom of school affirmations. The persistent quest for progress, combined with cultural assumptions, can add to increased feelings of anxiety and intensify high schooler apprehension.

Relational peculiarities, another ortho obstacle, assume a urgent part in forming the juvenile experience. The exchange among guardians and teens is full of pressure as the requirement for autonomy conflicts with parental power. Miscommunication, contrasting assumptions, and the battle for independence can make an unpredictable air inside the nuclear family, further powering youngster tension. Exploring these familial ortho obstacles requires open correspondence, sympathy, and an eagerness to connect the age hole.

Web-based entertainment, a generally late expansion to the ortho obstacles, intensifies the difficulties of pre-adulthood. The virtual world, with its organized pictures and consistent examination, turns into a favorable place for frailties and a misshaped feeling of the real world. The strain to adjust to online goals and the feeling of dread toward passing up a major opportunity (FOMO) add to an increased insecurity and social detachment. Tending to the effect of virtual entertainment on high schooler tension requires a multi-layered approach that incorporates media proficiency, confidence building, and encouraging genuine associations disconnected.

Peer connections, while a principal part of pre-adulthood, can likewise present ortho obstacles when set apart by tormenting, peer pressure, or harmful elements. The requirement for acknowledgment and having a place can lead young people to think twice about values, surrendering to pessimistic impacts in a bid to fit in. Exploring these friend related ortho obstacles includes advancing a culture of sympathy, strength, and confidence to engage teens to pursue informed decisions and face hurtful companion elements.

Understanding youngster tension goes past recognizing it as a stage; it requires an extensive investigation of the complex factors that add to this profound choppiness. Developing agonies, molded by the complex exchange of inner and outer powers, structure the underpinning of youngster tension. Exploring the ortho obstacles implanted in training, relational peculiarities, virtual entertainment, and friend connections is vital for guide youths through this extraordinary excursion. By cultivating a steady climate that tends to the one of a kind difficulties of immaturity, society can enable youngsters to rise up out of the cover of high schooler tension as versatile, mindful people prepared to explore the intricacies of adulthood.

1. Definition and Manifestations
Definition and Indications of Youngster Tension

High schooler tension, a term that typifies the close to home choppiness experienced during youth, is a perplexing and multi-layered peculiarity. It is significant to dig into its definition and indications to acquire a nuanced comprehension of this unavoidable part of the young experience.

At its center, adolescent anxiety alludes to the uplifted profound responsiveness and pain that frequently go with the progress from youth to adulthood. It's anything but a clinical determination yet rather a conversational articulation that catches the serious profound states experienced by young people as they wrestle with different inside and outer difficulties. The expression "tension" itself begins from German, conveying a feeling of firmly established nervousness and misgiving, which suitably describes the close to home scene of youth.

Signs of high schooler tension are different and can appear in different parts of a young person's life, enveloping feelings, ways of behaving, and relational connections. One conspicuous appearance is emotional episodes, where youngsters might waver between outrageous ups and downs, driven by hormonal vacillations and the conflict under the surface for character. These emotional episodes add to a rollercoaster of feelings that can be confounding for both the young people themselves and everyone around them.

A typical close to home sign of high schooler tension is a feeling of existential disarray. Teenagers wrestle with inquiries concerning their character, reason, and future, adding to a significant feeling of vulnerability. This existential tension is intently attached to the course of self-revelation, as teens explore the unpredictable excursion of understanding what their identity is and where they fit into the bigger cultural structure.

Social indications of high schooler anxiety frequently incorporate resistance and insubordination. As youngsters look for independence and freedom, they might challenge authority figures, including guardians, educators, and different grown-ups. This defiant way of behaving isn't really an indication of disobedience for the wellbeing of its own however can be seen as a characteristic tendency to state singularity and test limits in the mission for self-definition.

Relational connections endure the worst part of high schooler tension, with correspondence breakdowns, clashes, and an expanded longing for peer endorsement.

The requirement for social acknowledgment and the apprehension about dismissal increase during youthfulness, prompting elevated aversion to saw insults and social uncertainties. Peer connections become a pot for profound turn of events, as young people explore the sensitive harmony between fitting in and remaining consistent with themselves.

Scholastic execution is another field where adolescent apprehension can show. The strain to succeed scholastically, combined with the vulnerability about future instructive and vocation ways, adds to pressure and nervousness. The apprehension about disappointment and the craving to live up to outer assumptions can be overpowering, adding an extra layer to the profound scene of puberty.

Self-perception concerns are predominant signs of youngster tension, especially in a general public that frequently glorifies specific actual properties. Teenagers, going through critical actual changes during adolescence, may wrestle with weaknesses about their appearance. The strain to adjust to cultural excellence principles, exacerbated by the impact of web-based entertainment, can add to body disappointment and low confidence.

Peer examination, enhanced by the unavoidable presence of web-based entertainment, is a particular sign of youngster tension in the computerized age. The consistent openness to organized pictures and ways of life on stages like Instagram and TikTok can encourage unreasonable assumptions and a mutilated feeling of the real world. This increased familiarity with peer accomplishments and encounters can escalate insecurities and add to the apprehension about passing up a major opportunity (FOMO).

Relational intricacies are not insusceptible to the appearances of high schooler tension. The journey for independence and the craving to lay out a different personality can prompt struggles with guardians and kin. Correspondence breakdowns, described by an apparent absence of grasping on the two sides, can strain familial connections, adding to the generally close to home choppiness experienced by teens.

It is critical to perceive that the appearances of high schooler apprehension are not uniform; rather, they change generally founded on individual characters, ecological elements, and social impacts. A few teens might incorporate their battles, prompting withdrawal and contemplation, while others might externalize their tension through expressive ways of behaving and close to home eruptions. Understanding the assorted manners by which adolescent apprehension shows is fundamental for making fitted ways to deal with help and mediation.

Generally, high schooler tension is a characteristic and necessary piece of the juvenile experience.

It emerges from the convergence of natural, mental, and social factors, all of which add to the perplexing embroidered artwork of feelings and difficulties looked by young people. Perceiving and approving these signs is the most important move toward encouraging a strong climate that recognizes the intricacies of pre-adulthood and engages teens to explore this groundbreaking stage with versatility and mindfulness.

2. **Impact on Physical and Mental Well-being**
Influence on Physical and Mental Prosperity of Adolescent Tension

The wild excursion through immaturity, set apart by the recurring patterns of youngster apprehension, leaves a permanent engraving on both the physical and mental prosperity of teens. This vital period of improvement isn't just a close to home rollercoaster yet a powerful interchange of mental and physiological changes that significantly impact a young person's general wellbeing. Understanding the effect of youngster apprehension on physical and mental prosperity is fundamental for contriving techniques to help youths in exploring this extraordinary period.

Actual Prosperity:

One of the essential roads through which adolescent tension shows its effect on actual prosperity is rest interruption. The turbulent profound scene of youthfulness, combined with scholarly tensions and social elements, can add to sporadic rest designs. Lack of sleep, a typical outcome of high schooler tension, has flowing consequences for actual wellbeing, including compromised safe capability, debilitated mental execution, and disturbances in hormonal guideline. The fragile harmony between the requests of school, public activity, and the conflict under the surface for personality frequently prompts late evenings and inconsistent rest plans, intensifying the actual cost of youngster apprehension.

The hormonal variances intrinsic in youth additionally add to changes in craving and eating designs. For certain youngsters, stress and nervousness related with adolescent tension might bring about profound eating or loss of craving. These variances in eating ways of behaving can have suggestions for wholesome admission and may add to long haul wellbeing concerns like heftiness or hunger. The effect of youngster apprehension on dietary propensities highlights the multifaceted connection between profound prosperity and actual wellbeing during this developmental transformative phase.

Actual work, a foundation of wellbeing and prosperity, can be both a loss and a survival strategy with regards to youngster tension. A few youngsters, overpowered by the profound choppiness, may pull out from proactive tasks, prompting a stationary way of life.

Then again, others might channel their tension into extraordinary actual pursuits for of adapting or self-articulation. Finding some kind of harmony between actual work and the close to home requests of puberty is pivotal for advancing all encompassing prosperity.

Substance misuse is a huge concern connected to the effect of youngster tension on actual wellbeing. The longing to get away or numb the force of feelings might drive a few teens toward trial and error with medications and liquor. Substance misuse acts quick wellbeing takes a chance with like well as have long haul outcomes on mental health and generally speaking actual prosperity.

Understanding the relationship between's adolescent tension and the gamble of substance misuse is essential for carrying out preventive measures and giving suitable mediations.

Mental Prosperity:

The effect of adolescent tension on mental prosperity is maybe most articulated, given the perplexing transaction of profound, mental, and social variables during pre-adulthood. Uneasiness and sadness are predominant psychological well-being difficulties that frequently combine with the signs of adolescent anxiety. The steady strain to measure up to cultural assumptions, combined with the inward journey for self-character, can make a favorable place for psychological wellness battles.

The scholastic scene, set apart by elevated contest and assumptions, turns into a milestone for the psychological prosperity of young people encountering tension. The apprehension about disappointment, execution tension, and the steady quest for flawlessness add to pressure and can finish in emotional well-being problems. Perceiving the harmonious connection between scholarly tensions and high schooler anxiety is vital for carrying out steady instructive conditions that focus on both accomplishment and mental prosperity.

Self-perception concerns, intrinsic in the appearances of adolescent anxiety, further add to psychological wellness challenges. Young people, besieged by cultural magnificence principles and the steady examination worked with by online entertainment, may foster pessimistic self-perception discernments. Body disappointment, combined with the craving to adjust to ridiculous standards, can prompt the improvement of dietary problems, for example, anorexia nervosa or bulimia. Tending to the effect of youngster tension on self-perception requires a comprehensive methodology that includes both individual and cultural points of view.

Confidence, a foundation of mental prosperity, is unpredictably attached to the indications of high schooler tension. The unseen conflict for character and the outside tensions to adjust can dissolve self-assurance and add to insecurities. Fabricating and supporting confidence during youth is a preventive measure against the negative emotional well-being ramifications of high schooler tension, enabling teens to confront difficulties with strength and a positive mental self view.

Social connections, a basic part of youthfulness, bear a huge brunt regarding mental prosperity. Peer elements, set apart by the longing for acknowledgment and the feeling of dread toward dismissal, can add to social uneasiness and a feeling of segregation. Tormenting and peer pressure further compound the difficulties of social connections, establishing an unfriendly climate that adversely influences emotional wellness. Encouraging sound correspondence, compassion, and strength notwithstanding friendly difficulties is fundamental for relieving the emotional wellness cost of youngster anxiety.

Relational peculiarities, while persuasive in molding the emotionally supportive network for young people, can likewise add to psychological wellness challenges. Correspondence breakdowns, clashes over independence, and an apparent absence of understanding can strain familial connections, compounding the close to home disturbance experienced by young people. Perceiving the job of relational peculiarities in the psychological prosperity of young people is essential for carrying out mediations that advance open correspondence and common comprehension.

Self-destructive ideation, while an outrageous sign, is a sobering truth of the effect of high schooler tension on emotional wellness. The mind-boggling profound misery, combined with a feeling of sadness and disconnection, can push a few teens to mull over self destruction as an apparent getaway from their battles. Understanding the gamble factors and cautioning signs related with self-destructive ideation is basic for carrying out preventive measures and giving convenient psychological wellness support.

3. **Importance of Addressing Teen Angst**

Significance of Tending to Youngster Apprehension

The turbulent scene of youth, set apart by the complicated dance of feelings and difficulties epitomized in youngster anxiety, highlights the basic significance of tending to this peculiarity. A long way from being a momentary stage, youngster tension has significant ramifications for the all encompassing improvement of people during this groundbreaking period. Perceiving the meaning of tending to youngster tension is essential for encouraging a strong climate that enables teens to explore the intricacies of pre-adulthood and arise as versatile, mindful people.

One principal justification behind tending to youngster apprehension lies in its immediate relationship with emotional well-being results. The signs of youngster tension, including nervousness, discouragement, and self-destructive ideation, can enduringly affect a teen's psychological prosperity.

Untreated psychological wellness challenges during immaturity can make way for long haul battles, affecting scholar and vocation directions, relational connections, and generally speaking life fulfillment. By tending to adolescent anxiety proactively, society can add to the avoidance of emotional well-being problems and the advancement of positive mental prosperity in the urgent early stages.

Scholarly achievement and instructive fulfillment are characteristically connected to the significance of tending to high schooler tension. The tensions related with scholarly execution, frequently interweaved with the indications of youngster anxiety, can make a pattern of pressure and underachievement. Youngsters exploring the intricacies of puberty require an instructive climate that encourages scholarly development as well as focuses on their profound prosperity. Tending to youngster tension with regards to training includes executing steady strategies, sustaining a positive school culture, and giving assets to emotional wellness mindfulness and mediation.

The effect of youngster anxiety reaches out past the person to the cultural level. Neglected youngster tension can add to a scope of social issues, including substance misuse, misconduct, and relational struggles. The craving to get away from the power of feelings might drive a few teens toward unsafe ways of behaving, prompting long haul ramifications for both the people and the networks they have a place with. Tending to adolescent apprehension is, thusly, an interest in the social texture, advancing the prosperity of people and adding to the formation of better, stronger networks.

The nuclear family, a foundation of cultural construction, is significantly impacted by the significance of tending to high schooler tension. Relational peculiarities can either intensify or relieve the difficulties of youth, making it basic to address youngster anxiety inside the familial setting. Open correspondence, understanding, and backing from relatives assume a urgent part in assisting young people with exploring their close to home scene. By tending to high schooler tension inside the family, society adds to the making of a steady starting point for people to serious areas of strength for foster abilities, versatility, and a feeling of having a place.

Besides, tending to adolescent apprehension is fundamental for encouraging positive relational connections, both during pre-adulthood and in the years that follow. The difficulties of social connections during this period, set apart by peer elements, heartfelt interests, and advancing fellowships, can altogether shape a singular's capacity to frame significant associations sometime down the road. By giving direction and support to explore these difficulties, society lays the preparation for the advancement of solid relational abilities, compassion, and the capacity to lay out and keep up with positive connections.

The significance of tending to high schooler apprehension is highlighted by its effect on confidence and mental self portrait.

Young people, wrestling with the inward journey for character and outer tensions to adjust, are especially defenseless against variances in confidence. Ignored high schooler tension can add to a negative mental self portrait, upsetting the improvement of a solid self-idea. By perceiving and approving the battles of pre-adulthood, society can assume a critical part in supporting confidence and engaging people to confront difficulties with certainty and versatility.

Tending to youngster apprehension is likewise fundamental for moderating the gamble of maladaptive survival strategies, for example, substance misuse and self-hurt. The craving to get away or numb the power of feelings might drive a few young people toward trial and error with medications and liquor. By giving elective survival techniques and cultivating versatility, society can lessen the commonness of substance misuse and advance better approaches to managing the difficulties of youthfulness.

Besides, tending to youngster apprehension is instrumental in advancing capacity to appreciate anyone on a profound level and mindfulness. Youth is a time of serious close to home turn of events, and understanding and dealing with feelings are significant abilities for exploring this stage effectively. By tending to adolescent anxiety, society adds to the development of the ability to understand anyone on a profound level, empowering people to perceive and direct their feelings, sympathize with others, and pursue informed choices in view of mindfulness.

The significance of tending to youngster apprehension is highlighted by its effect on cultural standards and values. Young people, as they continued looking for personality, assume a vital part in molding social stories and cultural standards. Neglected high schooler tension might add to the propagation of destructive beliefs, like poisonous manliness or ridiculous magnificence guidelines. By offering help and direction, society can engage youths to challenge and reshape cultural standards, encouraging a culture that embraces variety, inclusivity, and credibility.

Chapter 1

The Teenage Ortho Landscape

The High school Ortho Scene: Exploring Difficulties and Amazing open doors

The teen ortho scene, enveloping the heap difficulties and open doors intrinsic in immaturity, frames a mind boggling landscape that essentially shapes the formative direction of people. Ortho, got from the Greek word "orthos" signifying "straight" or "right," fills in as a similitude for the cultural, familial, and instructive assumptions that young people experience and should explore. Understanding the complex idea of the adolescent ortho scene is essential for offering fitted help and direction to teens as they wrestle with the requests of this extraordinary stage.

Instructive Ortho Obstacles:

One of the essential aspects of the teen ortho scene is the instructive territory, set apart by obstacles that can be both requesting and developmental. The progress from center school to secondary school delivers a large group of scholastic difficulties, heightened by cultural assumptions and the approaching phantom of school confirmations. The ortho obstacle of scholastic execution turns into a focal concentration, frequently impacting the self-esteem and certainty of teens.

The strain to succeed scholastically can prompt pressure and nervousness, compounding the close to home disturbance currently inborn in youthfulness. The high school ortho scene requests a fragile harmony between making scholarly progress and encouraging the all encompassing improvement of people. Perceiving the significance of tending to scholarly ortho obstacles includes establishing instructive conditions that focus on thorough coursework as well as the psychological and close to home prosperity of understudies.

The cutthroat idea of current schooling can fuel ortho obstacles, pushing young people toward a persevering quest for flawlessness. The feeling of dread toward disappointment turns into a considerable hindrance, impacting direction, objective setting, and by and large prosperity. Exploring instructive ortho obstacles requires a change in outlook, underscoring the characteristic benefit of learning, self-awareness, and the improvement of decisive reasoning abilities over a thin spotlight on grades and state sanctioned test scores.

Family Ortho Elements:

Inside the familial domain, the ortho scene is set apart by the exchange of assumptions, correspondence breakdowns, and the mission for independence. The change from youth to puberty frequently achieves a renegotiation of the parent-teen relationship, where the ortho obstacle of offsetting parental direction with the requirement for freedom becomes articulated.

Ortho obstacles inside the nuclear family might appear as clashes over curfews, dynamic independence, and way of life decisions. The conflict between ages, established in contrasting points of view and encounters, highlights the significance of open correspondence and shared understanding. Tending to family ortho elements includes cultivating a climate where young people feel appreciated and upheld while guardians explore the fragile harmony among direction and permitting space for individual development.

The cultural ortho assumptions put on families likewise add to the ortho scene, with the strain to adjust to cultural standards and values. These assumptions might impact nurturing styles, vocation decisions, and the meaning of progress. Perceiving and testing cultural ortho assumptions inside the nuclear family is fundamental for establishing a climate that permits youngsters to investigate their personalities, interests, and values genuinely.

Web-based Entertainment Ortho Impacts:

A moderately late expansion to the teen ortho scene is the unavoidable impact of web-based entertainment. The computerized domain, with its organized pictures and steady examination, turns into a strong ortho force forming the discernments and ways of behaving of young people. The ortho obstacle of squeezing into online standards and the feeling of dread toward passing up a major opportunity (FOMO) add to a misshaped feeling of the real world and increased prevailing difficulties.

The effect of web-based entertainment ortho impacts stretches out past mental self portrait worries to include issues of cyberbullying, online provocation, and the obscuring of limits between the virtual and genuine universes. Tending to web-based entertainment ortho impacts requires a multi-pronged methodology that incorporates media proficiency training, the advancement of sound web-based ways of behaving, and the development of flexibility to endure the tensions of the computerized scene.

Peer Ortho Elements:

Peer connections structure a basic part of the teen ortho scene, introducing the two difficulties and valuable open doors for young people. The craving for acknowledgment and having a place frequently drives young people to explore the ortho obstacles of friend strain, harassing, and the need to adjust to cultural norms inside their groups of friends. The ortho elements of companion connections shape the profound and social improvement of young people, impacting their confidence, navigation, and generally prosperity.

Exploring peer ortho elements includes the development of decisiveness, sympathy, and the capacity to go with informed decisions. Building a strong companion climate that values variety, inclusivity, and realness mitigates the negative ortho impacts that might emerge from poisonous kinships or the strain to adjust to destructive normal practices. Peer connections, when explored effectively, can turn into a wellspring of solidarity, versatility, and shared development during the wild excursion through puberty.

Ortho Obstacles in Private Personality:

Fundamental to the young ortho scene is the inner turmoil for individual character. Young people wrestle with inquiries of self-revelation, reason, and characterizing their place inside the more extensive cultural structure. The ortho obstacle of adjusting individual personality to cultural assumptions and standards turns into an imposing test, adding to the close to home disturbance normal for youth.

The cultural ortho assumptions about orientation jobs, profession decisions, and social personality can shape the ortho obstacles that youngsters experience as they continued looking for self-definition. The significance of tending to ortho obstacles in private character includes making comprehensive spaces that celebrate variety, permitting youngsters to investigate and embrace their credible selves unafraid of judgment or dismissal.

Flexibility as a Reaction to Ortho Difficulties:

The high school ortho scene, with its heap difficulties, requires the development of strength as a reaction. Strength enables teens to explore ortho obstacles with flexibility, persistence, and a positive mentality. Instructive foundations, families, and networks assume a significant part in cultivating versatility by giving a steady system that recognizes the difficulties of youthfulness while supporting the inborn qualities of people.

Building versatility includes advancing a development outlook, empowering critical thinking abilities, and underscoring the significance of taking care of oneself and mental prosperity. By tending to ortho obstacles from the perspective of versatility, society adds to the improvement of people who can endure the difficulties of pre-adulthood as well as arise more grounded, more mindful, and better prepared to explore the intricacies of adulthood.

1.1 Overview of Orthopedic Issues in Adolescence

Muscular Issues in Youthfulness: Exploring Development and Advancement

The time of youthfulness, spreading over the progress from adolescence to adulthood, is a basic stage set apart by fast development, actual turn of events, and the rise of individual personality. Inside the more extensive setting of wellbeing contemplations, muscular issues assume a huge part in molding the prosperity of young people. These issues, going from outer muscle conditions to development related difficulties, highlight the significance of understanding and tending to muscular worries during this essential phase of life.

Development Related Muscular Worries:

One of the characterizing elements of pre-adulthood is the quick development and improvement that happens during adolescence. This period is portrayed by huge changes in bone length, bulk, and in general body organization. While most of youths experience development without huge muscular issues, certain worries might emerge, especially in situations where development is lopsided or happens at a sped up rate.

Scoliosis, a sidelong bend of the spine, is a typical development related muscular issue that frequently arises during puberty. The unique changes in the outer muscle framework can prompt the improvement of a bended spine, influencing stance and possibly causing uneasiness. Early recognition and mediation, like propping or exercise based recuperation, are significant for tending to scoliosis and forestalling further movement.

Another development related muscular concern is the event of development plate wounds. The development plates, situated close to the finishes of long bones, are defenseless during times of quick development. Wounds to these plates can upset ordinary bone turn of events and lead to long haul muscular issues. Appropriate finding and the executives, frequently including clinical management and exercise based recuperation, are fundamental for moderating the effect of development plate wounds on skeletal turn of events.

Sports-Related Muscular Wounds:

Youthfulness is when numerous people take part in coordinated sports and proactive tasks for the purpose of advancing wellness, socialization, and expertise improvement. In any case, the expanded support in sports likewise hoists the gamble of muscular wounds. Sports-related wounds in youth frequently include the outer muscle framework, including bones, joints, tendons, and muscles.

One normal muscular issue in this setting is front cruciate tendon (leg tendon) wounds. The leg tendon, a tendon in the knee, is powerless to injury during exercises that include unexpected stops, shifts in course, or hard impacts to the knee. Leg tendon wounds can be especially trying for young people, requiring brief clinical consideration and restoration to guarantee ideal recuperation and forestall long haul joint issues.

Abuse wounds, emerging from dreary weight on a specific piece of the body, are likewise common among juvenile competitors. Stress breaks, tendonitis, and development plate wounds can result from the combined effect of dreary movements, particularly in sports that underline explicit muscle gatherings or joint developments. Legitimate preparation strategies, sufficient rest, and suitable clinical oversight are fundamental for forestalling and overseeing abuse wounds.

Formative Muscular Problems:

Youthfulness is a period during which certain formative muscular problems might turn out to be more obvious or present new difficulties. Conditions like Legg-Calvé-Perthes sickness, slipped capital femoral epiphysis (SCFE), and Osgood-Schlatter illness are instances of issues that might show or advance during the young adult years.

Legg-Calvé-Perthes infection influences the hip joint, prompting the impermanent disturbance of blood stream to the femoral head. This interference can bring about the degeneration of the hip joint and cause agony and restricted portability. Early determination and mediation, frequently including propping or surgeries, are significant for dealing with the effect of Legg-Calvé-Perthes illness on hip turn of events.

Slipped capital femoral epiphysis is a condition where the ball at the upper finish of the thigh bone sneaks off the hip joint. This issue can prompt agony, restricted hip development, and a modified step. Convenient acknowledgment and adjustment of the impacted joint are fundamental to forestall further uprooting and limit long haul entanglements.

Osgood-Schlatter sickness is portrayed by aggravation and agony at the site where the patellar ligament joins to the tibia. This condition frequently emerges during development sprays when the bones and muscles are creating at various rates. While Osgood-Schlatter illness commonly settle with time and moderate administration, it features the interconnectedness of development and muscular worries during puberty.

Muscular Contemplations in Sports Specialization:

The pattern toward sports specialization, where youthful competitors center around a solitary game all year, has acquired unmistakable quality lately.

While specialization can prompt high level ability advancement, it likewise raises muscular worries, especially connected with abuse wounds and burnout. Teenagers taking part in sports specialization might confront an expanded gamble of pressure breaks, muscle awkward nature, and close to home weariness.

The redundant idea of sports specialization can overburden explicit joints and muscle gatherings, prompting lopsided characteristics and muscular issues. Also, the mental pressure related with serious preparation regimens and execution assumptions might add to mental weariness and effect in general prosperity.

Tending to muscular contemplations in sports specialization includes embracing a comprehensive methodology that focuses on rest, broadly educating, and mental help. Times of rest and broadening of proactive tasks can assist with forestalling abuse wounds and advance in general outer muscle wellbeing. Besides, cultivating a strong climate that stresses the significance of mental and profound prosperity is essential for moderating the likely unfortunate results of sports specialization.

Mechanical Effects on Muscular Wellbeing:

In the advanced age, the unavoidable utilization of innovation, especially cell phones and PCs, has suggestions for muscular wellbeing in pre-adulthood. Inordinate screen time and unfortunate ergonomics can add to outer muscle issues, including neck torment, shoulder strain, and stance related issues.

The pervasiveness of message neck, a condition portrayed by neck agony and harm to the spine coming about because of the delayed utilization of cell phones, features the muscular ramifications of innovative propensities. Teenagers, who frequently invest huge measures of energy on advanced gadgets, might be powerless against creating stance related muscular issues.

Advancing consciousness of legitimate ergonomics, empowering ordinary breaks from screen time, and integrating activities to reinforce the neck and back muscles are fundamental methodologies for tending to the muscular ramifications of innovation use. By encouraging sound propensities and careful gadget use, society can add to the counteraction of muscular issues related with the advanced age.

Psychosocial Effect of Muscular Issues:

Muscular issues in youthfulness reach out past the actual domain, affecting psychosocial prosperity and generally speaking personal satisfaction. Persistent torment, restrictions in versatility, and the requirement for clinical mediations can significantly affect the close to home and social parts of teenagers' lives.

Teenagers wrestling with muscular issues might encounter sensations of dissatisfaction, confinement, and a feeling of being not the same as their companions. The psychosocial effect of muscular difficulties can add to psychological well-being concerns, including nervousness and gloom. Tending to the psychosocial aspects of muscular issues includes a complete methodology that thinks about both the physical and close to home parts of juvenile prosperity.

Preventive Methodologies and Emotionally supportive networks:

Perceiving the diverse idea of muscular issues in youth, the execution of preventive methodologies and vigorous emotionally supportive networks is principal. Thorough muscular consideration includes a mix of mindfulness, early mediation, and continuous administration to address both formative and sports-related concerns.

Preventive measures incorporate ordinary outer muscle appraisals, mindfulness crusades on appropriate ergonomics and sports preparing procedures, and instructive drives focusing on youths, guardians, and mentors. Evaluating for scoliosis, observing development plate advancement, and advancing injury avoidance methodologies in sports are essential parts of preventive muscular consideration.

Emotionally supportive networks envelop a cooperative methodology including medical care experts, instructors, guardians, and mentors. Convenient distinguishing proof of muscular issues, combined with compelling correspondence and facilitated care, is fundamental for improving results. The coordination of exercise based recuperation, recovery, and psychosocial support adds to a comprehensive methodology that tends to the different components of muscular worries in youthfulness.

1.2 Common Ortho Challenges

Normal Muscular Difficulties: Exploring the Range of Outer muscle Issues

The domain of muscular health includes a huge swath of outer muscle conditions and difficulties that people might experience all through their lives. From intrinsic problems to degenerative circumstances and horrible wounds, muscular difficulties range a wide range, impacting the actual prosperity and personal satisfaction of those impacted. This investigation will dig into a portion of the normal muscular difficulties looked by people, featuring the intricacy of outer muscle wellbeing and the significance of exhaustive consideration.

Joint pain and Joint Issues:

Joint pain, a predominant muscular test, alludes to the irritation of at least one joints, prompting torment, enlarging, and firmness. Osteoarthritis, the most widely recognized structure, results from the mileage of joint ligament over the long haul. Rheumatoid joint inflammation, an immune system condition, includes the body's insusceptible framework going after the joints, causing aggravation.

These circumstances altogether influence joint capability and can prompt versatility limits. The aggravation related with joint pain can influence day to day exercises and lessen in general personal satisfaction. The board techniques for joint inflammation might incorporate meds, non-intrusive treatment, way of life alterations, and at times, careful intercessions like joint substitution.

Past joint inflammation, different joint problems add to muscular difficulties. Conditions like bursitis, tendonitis, and tendon wounds influence the designs encompassing joints, causing torment and utilitarian impedance. Convenient analysis and suitable mediations, going from rest and non-intrusive treatment to surgeries, are fundamental for tending to joint issues and saving outer muscle capability.

Cracks and Horrible Wounds:

Horrendous wounds, including breaks, disengagements, and delicate tissue wounds, comprise a huge class of muscular difficulties. Cracks, or broken bones, can result from falls, sports wounds, or mishaps. The seriousness of breaks fluctuates, going from straightforward cracks that might mend with immobilization to complex breaks requiring careful mediation.

The administration of cracks includes realignment of the wrecked bone, immobilization through projecting or supporting, and restoration to reestablish strength and capability. In extreme cases, open decrease and inward obsession (ORIF) might be important to balance out the break.

Separations happen when the closures of bones are constrained out of their ordinary situations inside a joint. This can result from high-influence injury or dreary pressure. Brief decrease of the disengaged joint and restoration are essential to forestall long haul intricacies and guarantee ideal recuperation.

Delicate tissue wounds, like injuries and strains, include harm to muscles, tendons, and ligaments. These wounds frequently result from abuse, unexpected developments, or injury. Rest, ice, pressure, and height (RICE) are generally utilized for introductory administration, trailed by exercise based recuperation to work with mending and forestall repetitive wounds.

Spinal Circumstances:

The spine, an intricate construction of vertebrae, circles, and supporting tendons, is helpless to different muscular difficulties. Degenerative plate sickness, herniated circles, and spinal stenosis are normal circumstances influencing the spine.

Degenerative plate infection includes the breakdown of intervertebral circles after some time, prompting torment, firmness, and decreased adaptability. Herniated circles happen when the inward center of a plate projects through its external layer, possibly causing nerve pressure and transmitting torment.

Spinal stenosis, portrayed by the restricting of the spinal waterway, can bring about tension on the spinal string and nerves, causing torment and neurological side effects.

The executives of spinal circumstances frequently includes a mix of moderate measures, like exercise based recuperation and torment the board, and careful intercessions when important. Spinal combination, laminectomy, and discectomy are among the surgeries utilized to resolve explicit spinal issues.

Scoliosis:

Scoliosis, a horizontal bend of the spine, ordinarily arises during immaturity. While certain cases are gentle and may not need mediation, serious scoliosis can affect lung capability and lead to agony and distortion. Early discovery through routine screening is vital for observing the movement of scoliosis and carrying out fitting mediations, which might incorporate propping or careful revision.

The administration of scoliosis underscores the rectification of spinal arch as well as the protection of lung capability and by and large spinal wellbeing. Standard checking, active recuperation, and, in extreme cases, spinal combination medical procedure are fundamental parts of scoliosis the executives.

Sports-Related Wounds:

Support in sports and proactive tasks, while useful for by and large wellbeing, likewise represents the gamble of muscular wounds. Competitors might encounter a scope of outer muscle issues, including tendon tears, ligament wounds, and stress breaks.

Front cruciate tendon (upper leg tendon) wounds, normal in sports that include turning and abrupt stops, can essentially affect knee strength. Remaking a medical procedure and restoration are in many cases important to reestablish knee capability and forestall long haul confusions.

Ligament wounds, like Achilles ligament breaks or rotator sleeve tears, can result from abuse or intense injury. These wounds might require careful intercession and broad recovery to recapture strength and capability.

Stress cracks, pervasive in exercises that include dull effect, can influence bones like the shin or foot. Rest, adjustment of movement, and progressive re-visitation of activity are fundamental parts of overseeing pressure breaks.

Innate and Formative Problems:

Muscular difficulties can likewise emerge from inherent or formative circumstances that influence the outer muscle framework. Conditions like clubfoot, hip dysplasia, and innate appendage anomalies might require early mediation to improve outer muscle advancement.

Clubfoot, described by a disfigurement in the arrangement of the foot, frequently requires projecting or supporting to address the position slowly. Now and again, careful adjustment might be vital.

Hip dysplasia, a condition where the hip joint doesn't grow as expected, may require mediations, for example, outfits or medical procedure to work with legitimate joint arrangement and forestall long haul issues like osteoarthritis.

Innate appendage irregularities, like appendage length errors or anomalies in bone turn of events, may require careful mediations, orthotic gadgets, or prosthetics to help ideal capability and versatility.

Abuse Wounds:

Abuse wounds result from dull weight on a particular piece of the body without sufficient time for recuperation. These wounds are normal in exercises that include tedious movements or high-influence pressure, like running, cycling, or particular sorts of preparing.

Abuse wounds incorporate a range of conditions, including pressure cracks, tendonitis, and stress responses. Legitimate preparation procedures, sufficient rest, and continuous movement in power are pivotal for forestalling abuse wounds. At the point when these wounds happen, ideal intercession, rest, and recovery are fundamental to advance mending and forestall repetitive issues.

Heftiness Related Muscular Issues:

The rising predominance of heftiness is a critical supporter of muscular difficulties. Overabundance body weight puts extra weight on joints, especially in the knees and hips, prompting an expanded gamble of osteoarthritis. People with weight may likewise encounter outer muscle issues connected with modified biomechanics and expanded aggravation.

The administration of muscular issues connected with corpulence includes a multi-layered approach that incorporates weight the executives, work out, and non-intrusive treatment. Bariatric medical procedure might be viewed as in situations where huge weight reduction is important to mitigate muscular side effects.

Geriatric Muscular Difficulties:

As people age, the outer muscle framework goes through changes that add to muscular difficulties. Osteoporosis, a condition described by diminished bone thickness, expands the gamble of cracks, especially in the hip, spine, and wrist. Falls in the old populace can have extreme results, underscoring the significance of preventive measures and bone wellbeing support.

Joint pain, a diligent worry across the life expectancy, frequently turns out to be more articulated in more seasoned people, influencing joint capability and portability. The administration of geriatric muscular difficulties includes a mix of way of life changes, meds, and, when essential, careful intercessions to resolve outer muscle issues and upgrade personal satisfaction.

Ongoing Torment Disorders:

Ongoing torment disorders, including complex local agony condition (CRPS) and fibromyalgia, present novel muscular difficulties. CRPS, described by extreme torment and tangible changes, may foster following injury or injury. Fibromyalgia, a condition including inescapable outer muscle torment, weakness, and rest unsettling influences, requires an extensive methodology that tends to both physical and mental perspectives.

The administration of ongoing torment disorders includes a multidisciplinary approach, integrating torment the board techniques, non-intrusive treatment, and mental help. Customized mediations expect to further develop capability, reduce agony, and improve the general prosperity of people managing constant torment.

1.3 Factors Influencing Ortho Health in Teens

Factors Impacting Muscular Wellbeing in Youngsters: An Exhaustive Investigation

The muscular wellbeing of young people is impacted by a horde of elements that range organic, natural, and way of life aspects. As youths go through fast development, actual turn of events, and take part in different exercises, the exchange of these variables becomes significant in forming their outer muscle prosperity. Understanding the diverse idea of the effects on muscular wellbeing is vital for advancing ideal turn of events and forestalling expected issues during this basic phase of life.

Organic Variables:

1. **Development and Advancement:**

   The essential organic variable impacting muscular wellbeing in adolescents is the regular course of development and advancement. Immaturity is set apart by huge skeletal development, including the extending of bones and the advancement of muscle structure.

   This period is described by the combination of development plates, which are urgent for bone prolongation. The rate and example of development can change among people, impacting outer muscle arrangement and the gamble of specific muscular circumstances.

2. **Hereditary qualities:**

   Hereditary elements assume a significant part in deciding a singular's vulnerability to muscular circumstances. Certain circumstances, like scoliosis or innate appendage irregularities, may have a genetic part. Understanding the hereditary inclinations inside families considers proactive checking and early intercession when important.

3. **Hormonal Changes:**

Hormonal changes during pubescence add to the development of the outer muscle framework. The arrival of development chemical and sex chemicals impacts bone thickness, bulk, and by and large body structure. Hormonal vacillations can influence tendon and ligament laxity, influencing joint soundness. These organic changes highlight the significance of perceiving the interconnectedness of hormonal variables with muscular wellbeing in youngsters.

Natural Variables:

1. **Actual work and Sports Support:**
   The level and sort of active work essentially impact muscular wellbeing in teens. Normal, weight-bearing exercises add to bone thickness and outer muscle strength. Notwithstanding, cooperation in specific games or exercises that include dull pressure or high-influence developments might build the gamble of wounds, for example, stress breaks or tendon injuries. Offsetting active work with legitimate preparation procedures and satisfactory rest is fundamental for advancing outer muscle wellbeing.

2. **Natural Ergonomics:**
   The climate wherein youngsters invest a lot of energy, including home and school settings, can influence muscular wellbeing. Poor ergonomic practices, for example, inaccurate work area level or delayed times of screen time with ill-advised pose, may add to outer muscle issues, including neck agony and back strain. Tending to natural variables through ergonomic changes can assume a preventive part in muscular wellbeing.

3. **Financial Variables:**

Financial elements, including admittance to medical services, instructive open doors, and sporting offices, can impact muscular wellbeing in adolescents. People from lower financial foundations might confront hindrances to preventive medical care, opportune mediation for muscular issues, and support in coordinated sports or proactive tasks. Tending to these differences is essential for guaranteeing evenhanded muscular wellbeing results.

Social and Way of life Variables:

1. **Nourishment:**
   Sufficient sustenance is principal for supporting ideal outer muscle improvement in adolescents. Calcium, vitamin D, and other fundamental supplements are significant for bone wellbeing. Dietary lacks during youthfulness can think twice about thickness and increment the gamble of conditions like osteoporosis in later life. Empowering a decent eating regimen wealthy in supplements is fundamental for cultivating muscular wellbeing.

2. **Weight The board:**
   Keeping a sound weight is essential to muscular wellbeing in teenagers. Abundance body weight puts extra weight on joints, especially in weight-bearing regions like the knees and hips. Stoutness is related with an expanded gamble of muscular circumstances, including osteoarthritis and stress cracks. Advancing solid way of life decisions, including customary actual work and a decent eating routine, adds to weight the executives and outer muscle prosperity.

3. **Rest Examples:**
   Sufficient rest is fundamental for in general wellbeing, including outer muscle prosperity. During rest, the body goes through cycles of fix and development, significant for keeping up with the honesty of bones, muscles, and connective tissues. Unfortunate rest designs or insufficient rest might think twice about body's capacity to recuperate from everyday exercises and add to outer muscle weariness.

4. **Stance and Body Mechanics:**

Appropriate stance and body mechanics are fundamental for muscular wellbeing. Mistaken body arrangement, particularly during exercises like sitting or lifting, can add to muscle awkward nature and stress on joints. Teaching adolescents on the significance of good stance and giving direction on ergonomic practices in everyday exercises add to the counteraction of muscular issues.

Psychosocial Elements:

1. **Emotional wellness:**
   Psychosocial factors, including emotional wellness and close to home prosperity, assume a huge part in muscular wellbeing. Conditions, for example, misery and nervousness can affect torment insight and the capacity to stick to restoration programs. Moreover, stress might add to muscle pressure and outer muscle distress. Addressing psychological well-being concerns is vital to advancing comprehensive muscular prosperity.

2. **Peer Impact and Social Elements:**
   Peer impact and social elements inside the young adult populace can impact ways of behaving connected with muscular wellbeing. This might remember support for specific games, adherence to wellness patterns, or companion strain to take part in exercises that might present muscular dangers. Advancing a positive and steady friendly climate is fundamental for empowering solid way of life decisions.

3. **Self-perception and Confidence:**

Self-perception and confidence are entwined with muscular wellbeing in teenagers. Youths who are disappointed with their bodies might take part in ways of behaving that influence outer muscle prosperity, like unnecessary activity or unfortunate dietary practices. Encouraging a positive self-perception and elevating confidence add to better way of life decisions and by and large muscular wellbeing.

Preventive Measures and Mediation:

Understanding the large number of elements affecting muscular wellbeing in teenagers highlights the significance of preventive measures and convenient mediation. Extensive outer muscle evaluations, including hereditary inclination contemplations, can help with proactive observing and early discovery of possible issues.

Instructive drives focusing on the two youngsters and their guardians are pivotal for advancing solid ways of behaving and way of life decisions. This remembers giving data to appropriate sustenance, the advantages of active work, ergonomic practices, and the significance of mental prosperity in muscular wellbeing.

Admittance to medical care administrations and preventive muscular consideration is fundamental for resolving issues instantly and executing mediations when vital. Normal outer muscle screenings, especially during development sprays, can help with the early ID of conditions like scoliosis or formative anomalies.

Restoration and active recuperation programs custom fitted to the interesting necessities of youngsters add to ideal recuperation from wounds and the improvement of solidarity and adaptability. Accentuating the significance of rest, particularly with regards to sports support, is imperative for forestalling abuse wounds and guaranteeing outer muscle versatility.

Advancing value in muscular wellbeing includes tending to financial variations and giving assets that empower all young people to get to preventive consideration and mediations. This incorporates drives to make sports and proactive tasks available to people from assorted financial foundations.

1.4 Long-term Effects of Untreated Ortho Problems

Long haul Impacts of Untreated Muscular Issues: Disentangling the Effect on Outer muscle Wellbeing

Untreated muscular issues in the long haul can apply a significant and frequently flowing effect on a person's outer muscle wellbeing. From ongoing agony and versatility issues to the potential for degenerative circumstances, the outcomes of ignoring muscular worries can reach out a long ways past the underlying side effects. This investigation digs into the many-sided snare of long haul impacts that untreated muscular issues can apply on people, stressing the significance of proactive intercession and thorough muscular consideration.

Constant Torment and Distress:

One of the most prompt and industrious outcomes of untreated muscular issues is the advancement of constant torment and uneasiness. Whether coming from conditions like joint inflammation, untreated cracks, or tendon wounds, persevering torment can essentially decrease a singular's personal satisfaction. Persistent agony influences actual prosperity as well as negatively affects emotional well-being, adding to pressure, nervousness, and even gloom.

Untreated muscular issues can prompt the advancement of optional issues, like muscle awkward nature and compensatory developments, which further compound agony. For instance, an untreated knee injury might bring about changed stride designs, overwhelming different joints like the hips and lower back. Over the long run, this cascading type of influence can make a pattern of ongoing agony and uneasiness that turns out to be progressively difficult to break.

Joint Degeneration and Osteoarthritis:

Inability to resolve muscular issues quickly may make ready for joint degeneration, especially in weight-bearing joints like the knees, hips, and spine. The delayed weight on joints because of misalignments, untreated wounds, or constant irritation can speed up the mileage of ligament — a defensive tissue that pads the finishes of bones in joints.

As ligament disintegrates, bones might begin to rub against one another, causing agony, enlarging, and solidness normal for osteoarthritis. Osteoarthritis is a degenerative joint sickness that can significantly affect versatility and capability. The dynamic idea of this condition implies that people might encounter a slow decrease in joint wellbeing, restricting their capacity to perform day to day exercises and reducing by and large personal satisfaction.

Restricted Scope of Movement and Utilitarian Disabilities:

Untreated muscular issues frequently lead to constraints in scope of movement and practical debilitations. Whether because of untreated cracks, joint contractures, or delicate tissue wounds, the inability to resolve these issues can bring about long haul ramifications for portability and actual abilities.

For example, an ignored ligament injury or untreated muscle irregular characteristics can prompt a limited scope of movement in a joint. After some time, this restriction might become super durable, influencing a singular's capacity to perform straightforward errands like coming to, bowing, or lifting. Practical hindrances can stretch out to exercises of everyday living, affecting freedom and requiring versatile techniques for following through with routine responsibilities.

Muscle Decay and Shortcoming:

The exchange between untreated muscular issues and the outer muscle framework frequently includes a mind boggling relationship with the muscles. Constant agony and decreased versatility can prompt neglect of specific muscles, bringing about muscle decay and shortcoming. The neglect of muscles because of modified development examples or evasion of difficult exercises can make a pattern of deconditioning.

Muscle decay decreases strength as well as adds to joint precariousness and further compounds muscular issues. Debilitated muscles are less ready to offer sufficient help to joints, expanding the gamble of falls and extra wounds. Tending to muscular worries sooner rather than later is essential for protecting muscle strength and forestalling the auxiliary confusions related with muscle decay.

Postural Irregularities and Modified Biomechanics:

Untreated muscular issues can lead to postural irregularities and changed biomechanics, which, thusly, add to a large group of long haul outer muscle issues. For instance, untreated scoliosis — a horizontal shape of the spine — can prompt postural uneven characters that influence the whole outer muscle framework.

Postural irregularities might bring about lopsided appropriation of powers on joints and delicate tissues, inclining people toward abuse wounds and degenerative changes. Modified biomechanics can likewise put weight on adjoining structures, prompting compensatory developments and awkward nature that propagate muscular issues. Interceding ahead of schedule to address postural irregularities and reestablish appropriate biomechanics is fundamental for forestalling the drawn out results related with these issues.

Neurological Inconveniences:

Certain muscular issues, whenever left untreated, may lead to neurological difficulties. For example, untreated spinal circumstances, for example, herniated circles or spinal stenosis can apply tension on the spinal line or nerves, prompting neurological side effects. These side effects might incorporate transmitting torment, deadness, shivering, and muscle shortcoming.

After some time, industrious pressure of nerves can prompt more extreme neurological shortfalls, influencing engine capability and tactile insight. Ideal mediation, remembering careful decompression for specific cases, is pivotal for forestalling the movement of neurological complexities related with untreated muscular issues.

Psychosocial Effect and Diminished Personal satisfaction:

The drawn out results of untreated muscular issues stretch out past the actual domain, affecting a person's psychosocial prosperity and generally speaking personal satisfaction. Ongoing torment, restricted portability, and utilitarian debilitations can add to sensations of dissatisfaction, confinement, and a feeling of reliance.

People wrestling with untreated muscular issues might encounter difficulties in friendly and sporting exercises, prompting a lessened feeling of cooperation and commitment. The psychosocial effect of untreated muscular issues can add to emotional wellness concerns, including tension and melancholy, making a cycle where close to home prosperity is complicatedly connected with actual wellbeing.

Decreased personal satisfaction might stretch out to proficient and instructive circles, influencing a singular's capacity to perform work obligations or participate in scholastic pursuits. The constraints forced by untreated muscular issues can have sweeping ramifications for a singular's general life fulfillment and satisfaction.

Difficulties in Muscular Medical procedures:

In situations where muscular issues at last brief the requirement for careful mediation, postponing treatment can present extra intricacies and dangers. For instance, joint substitution medical procedures, like hip or knee substitutions, may turn out to be really difficult assuming there is critical joint degeneration or harm. Intricacies during medical procedure, delayed recuperation times, and improved probability of postoperative issues are expected results of deferring vital muscular techniques.

Untreated muscular issues may likewise require greater careful intercessions than would have been required in the event that the issues had been tended to before. The seriousness of the muscular condition, combined with the potential for complexities, highlights the significance of opportune intercession to improve careful results and limit related gambles.

Monetary Weight and Medical care Expenses:

According to a more extensive point of view, untreated muscular issues can add to a critical monetary weight on people and the medical services framework. The drawn out administration of ongoing circumstances, restoration, and potential careful intercessions involve significant medical services costs. Roundabout expenses, including loss of efficiency and pay because of diminished work limit, add to the monetary effect related with untreated muscular issues.

The monetary weight reaches out past the person to cultural costs connected with handicap facilities, social help administrations, and the potential for long haul restoration. Resolving muscular issues sooner rather than later can relieve the monetary repercussions related with delayed and untreated outer muscle issues.

Chapter 2

The Anatomy of Teen Angst

The Life systems of Youngster Apprehension: Exploring the Tempestuous Landscape of Juvenile Feelings

The scene of youth is portrayed by a heap of feelings, difficulties, and self-disclosure, with youngster tension arising as a conspicuous and frequently complex part of this extraordinary period. The life systems of high schooler tension includes a nuanced investigation of mental, natural, and social factors that add to the close to home disturbance experienced by youngsters. Understanding the mind boggling elements of high schooler apprehension is pivotal for cultivating compassion, offering help, and advancing the close to home prosperity of youths as they explore the wild landscape of youthfulness.

Mental Aspects:

1. **Character Development:**
   Key to the life structures of youngster apprehension is the course of personality arrangement. Youths wrestle with inquiries of self-disclosure, endeavoring to produce a feeling of personality that lines up with their developing qualities, convictions, and yearnings. The mission for personality frequently includes investigation, trial and error, and an increased consciousness of cultural assumptions.

   The strain to adjust to cultural standards while looking for credible self-articulation can add to struggles under the surface, producing anxiety as youngsters arrange the sensitive harmony among congruity and distinction.

2. **Close to home Power and Instability:**
   The young mind goes through huge neurological changes during youth, especially in the prefrontal cortex — the district liable for drive control, direction, and profound guideline. The improvement of these mental capabilities is a progressive cycle, prompting an impermanent irregularity between the close

to home and judicious parts of navigation. This neurobiological shift adds to the close to home power and unpredictability saw in young people, enhancing the experience of anxiety as they explore complex feelings and relational connections.

3. **Mental Turn of events and Point of view Taking:**
Mental advancement during pre-adulthood includes the refinement of dynamic reasoning and the capacity to participate in context taking. While this mental development encourages decisive reasoning, it additionally makes the way for increased mindfulness and thoughtfulness. Youths might wrestle with existential inquiries, contemplating their spot on the planet, the importance of life, and the vulnerability representing things to come. The investigation of existential subjects adds to a significant feeling of tension as teenagers face the intricacies of presence and endeavor to get a handle on their developing personalities.

4. **Social Examination and Companion Impact:**

The social elements of youth present a component of correlation and friend impact that adds to high schooler tension. Young people, anxious to lay out their social personalities, frequently participate in friendly examination — thinking about themselves in contrast to their companions in different spaces, including scholastics, appearance, and societal position. The craving for social acknowledgment and apprehension about dismissal can heighten serious insecurities, encouraging tension as teenagers explore the unpredictable social texture of puberty.

Organic Elements:

1. **Hormonal Variances:**
Hormonal variances, a sign of pre-adulthood, assume an essential part in the life systems of high schooler tension. The flood in chemicals, including estrogen and testosterone, impacts mind-set guideline and close to home reactions. Hormonal changes can add to mind-set swings, uplifted close to home reactivity, and a vulnerability to push. The interaction between hormonal changes and the creating cerebrum makes way for close to home disturbance, molding the profound scene of puberty.

2. **Mental health:**
The juvenile mind goes through a unique course of reworking and development. While the prefrontal cortex creates and upgrades chief capabilities, the limbic framework, answerable for feelings, encounters increased action. This formative imbalance between mental control and close to home handling can prompt hasty way of behaving, profound reactivity, and difficulties in close to home guideline. The continuous development of the cerebrum adds to the physical underpinning of high schooler anxiety.

3. **Rest Examples and Circadian Rhythms:**

Organic variables impacting rest designs and circadian rhythms assume a part in the sign of youngster tension. Teenagers frequently experience a change in circadian rhythms, bringing about an inclination for later sleep times and waking times. Unpredictable rest designs and inadequate rest can influence temperament, compound close to home reactivity, and add to sensations of crabbiness and dissatisfaction. The bidirectional connection among rest and close to home prosperity frames an organic supporting of high schooler tension.

Social and Natural Impacts:

1. **Peer Connections and Prevalent burdens:**
   The social component of puberty, set apart by the rising meaning of friend connections, presents both emotionally supportive networks and expected stressors. Peer connections assume a critical part in forming character, impacting ways of behaving, and offering profound help. Be that as it may, the longing for social acknowledgment can likewise prompt congruity, prevailing difficulties, and the anxiety toward prohibition. Arranging these elements adds to the social life systems of youngster anxiety.

2. **Relational intricacies and Independence:**
   The advancing elements inside the nuclear family add to the profound scene of pre-adulthood. As teens take a stab at expanded independence and freedom, clashes with guardians and kin might emerge. The pressure between the longing for independence and the requirement for familial help makes a complex profound landscape, encouraging sensations of disappointment, disobedience, and a mission for individual character inside the familial setting.

3. **Cultural Assumptions and Scholarly Tensions:**
   The more extensive cultural setting, including scholarly assumptions and cultural tensions, adds one more layer to the life structures of youngster apprehension. Young people frequently wrestle with the strain to succeed scholastically, settle on future-arranged choices, and adjust to cultural assumptions. The apprehension about missing the mark, combined with the vulnerability representing things to come, adds to elevated pressure and inner unrest as adolescents explore the requests of the scholarly world and cultural principles.

4. **Innovation and Online Entertainment Effect:**

The ubiquity of innovation and the impact of online entertainment further shape the social life structures of youngster tension. Teenagers are submerged in a computerized scene that amplifies social correlation, presents new types of social approval, and gives a stage to both positive and negative social cooperations. The effect of cyberbullying, the organized idea of online characters, and the steady availability add to the close to home intricacies of immaturity.

Ecological Stressors and Injury:

1. **Ecological Stressors:**
   Teens might confront natural stressors, including monetary insecurity, local area brutality, or blood related difficulties, that add to the life structures of high schooler anxiety. The outside pressures related with these stressors can fuel existing profound weaknesses, prompting uplifted tension, touchiness, and a feeling of frailty.

2. **Horrendous Encounters:**

Horrendous encounters, like physical or psychological mistreatment, disregard, or misfortune, can altogether influence the profound prosperity of teenagers. Unsettled injury might appear as extreme feelings, trouble confiding in others, and difficulties in shaping secure connections. The convergence of injury and the formative phase of immaturity enhances the close to home intricacies, adding to the life systems of high schooler anxiety.

Survival strategies and Versatility:

1. **Ways of dealing with hardship or stress and Versatile Systems:**
   The life structures of youngster tension likewise includes an investigation of ways of dealing with especially difficult times and versatile procedures utilized by teenagers. A few young people might foster sound strategies for dealing with hardship or stress, like looking for social help, participating in imaginative outlets, or rehearsing care. Others might go to less versatile systems, including substance use, self-damage, or evasion, for the purpose of dealing with profound pain. Understanding these survival techniques gives bits of knowledge into the manners in which adolescents explore the personal difficulties of youth.

2. **Flexibility and Positive Results:**

While adolescent anxiety includes battles and profound choppiness, perceiving the potential for versatility and positive outcomes is fundamental. Numerous youths, in spite of confronting difficulties, foster versatility through strong connections, self-revelation, and the development of adapting abilities. Strong people might outfit the energy of high schooler tension to fuel self-improvement, imagination, and the advancement of a hearty close to home tool stash.

Emotionally supportive networks and Mediation:
Perceiving the life structures of high schooler anxiety highlights the significance of emotionally supportive networks and opportune intercession. A comprehensive methodology includes encouraging open correspondence among young people and confided in grown-ups, giving places of refuge to articulation, and offering assets for profound prosperity. Emotional wellness training, destigmatizing help-chasing ways of behaving, and advancing a culture of compassion add to a steady climate for youths exploring the intricacies of youngster tension.

2.1 Psychological and Emotional Components

Mental and Profound Parts: Unwinding the Mind boggling Strings of Juvenile Emotional well-being

The mental and close to home parts of juvenile psychological wellness comprise a dynamic and perplexing embroidery that fundamentally shapes the prosperity of teens. The juvenile years, set apart by a hurricane of mental, profound, and social changes, request a nuanced investigation of the mental variables impacting emotional wellness. Understanding the complicated exchange of these parts is fundamental for encouraging strength, advancing positive psychological wellness results, and tending to the interesting difficulties that go with the excursion through youth.

Personality Arrangement and Self-Idea:

At the core of the mental parts of young adult psychological wellness lies the mind boggling course of personality arrangement. Young people wrestle with inquiries of self-revelation, endeavoring to manufacture a feeling of personality that lines up with their developing qualities, convictions, and desires. This mission for personality is complicatedly connected with the improvement of a positive self-idea — the insight people have of themselves.

The arrangement of character includes the combination of different aspects, including orientation character, social personality, and individual qualities. Young people explore cultural assumptions, peer impacts, and inward reflections as they develop a story that characterizes what their identity is. Positive encounters that certify an intelligent and positive self-idea add to vigorous psychological well-being, while unseen fits of turmoil or outer tensions can prompt increased weakness and profound trouble.

Profound Guideline and The capacity to appreciate individuals on a deeper level:

Profound guideline, a pivotal part of juvenile psychological well-being, includes the capacity to really oversee and regulate feelings. The adolescent mind goes through huge neurological changes, especially in the prefrontal cortex, which is liable for drive control and close to home guideline. The improvement of the capacity to understand people on a profound level — the capacity to perceive, comprehend, and deal with one's own feelings and those of others — assumes a critical part in psychological wellness results.

Young people with advanced profound guideline abilities are better prepared to explore the highs and lows of immaturity. They can adjust to stressors, express feelings in sound ways, and structure good connections. On the other hand, hardships in profound guideline might appear as emotional episodes, imprudent way of behaving, or close to home eruptions, adding to the close to home choppiness normal for youthfulness.

Mental Turn of events and Navigation:

The mental improvement of teenagers includes the refinement of conceptual reasoning, basic thinking, and thinking abilities. The development of the prefrontal cortex upgrades leader capabilities, permitting youngsters to take part in additional refined mental cycles. In any case, this mental development isn't uniform, prompting an impermanent irregularity between the profound and levelheaded parts of navigation.

Young people might wrestle with risk-taking ways of behaving, impulsivity, and the test of weighing transient awards against long haul results. The transaction between mental turn of events and profound reactivity adds to the intricacy of decision-production during youthfulness. Positive mental improvement encourages versatile critical thinking abilities, while moves in this domain can prompt expanded weakness to psychological wellness issues.

Social Examination and Friend Connections:

The social element of immaturity presents the mental part of social examination — the assessment of oneself in contrast with peers. Peer connections assume a focal part in molding social character, impacting ways of behaving, and offering close to home help. Be that as it may, the craving for social acknowledgment and the apprehension about dismissal can strengthen serious insecurities and add to the development of psychological wellness challenges.

Teenagers participate in friendly examination across different spaces, including scholastics, appearance, and societal position. Good friendly correlation can give inspiration and a feeling of having a place, however pessimistic social examination might prompt sensations of inadequacy and low confidence. Exploring the complicated elements of companion connections is a mental test that fundamentally impacts emotional wellness results during youth.

Independence and Relational peculiarities:

As young people make progress toward expanded independence and autonomy, the mental elements inside the nuclear family go through critical movements. The journey for independence includes laying out an identity separated from the family and arranging the harmony among freedom and familial help. This mental part adds to the close to home scene of youth.

Clashes with guardians and kin might emerge as teens attest their independence, prompting uplifted feelings and difficulties in correspondence. The mental requirement for freedom, combined with the craving for familial association, makes a fragile close to home territory.

Positive relational peculiarities that help independence while keeping a groundwork of consistent reassurance add to positive emotional well-being results, while stressed family connections might worsen mental weaknesses.

Existential Investigation and Future Direction:

The mental and mental improvement of teenagers incorporates an investigation of existential topics — inquiries concerning the significance of life, individual reason, and the vulnerability representing things to come. This investigation adds to the mental part of existential tension, a profound reflection on the intricacies of presence. Youths wrestle with inquiries regarding their spot on the planet, the quest for significant objectives, and the certainty of progress.

Existential investigation is intently attached to future direction — the ability to imagine and make arrangements for what's in store. The mental effect of mulling over the future, including instructive and vocation objectives, can impact psychological well-being. Positive future direction adds to a feeling of direction and inspiration, while existential tension might prompt uplifted pressure and inner unrest as teens stand up to the vulnerabilities of the excursion ahead.

Survival techniques and Versatility:

The mental domain of survival techniques and versatility assumes a crucial part in deciding how youths explore difficulties and stressors. Survival techniques are versatile procedures people use to oversee pressure, control feelings, and explore tough spots. The collection of survival techniques fluctuates among teenagers, for certain creating solid systems like looking for social help, participating in imaginative outlets, or rehearsing care.

Strength, a mental build, alludes to the capacity to return from difficulty, adjust to difficulties, and keep up with positive psychological well-being notwithstanding life's troubles. Teenagers who foster strength display an ability to endure pressure, gain from difficulties, and develop a feeling of organization in exploring their lives. Understanding and encouraging sound methods for dealing with especially difficult times and versatility add to positive mental results during youthfulness.

Psychosocial Stressors and Injury:

Psychosocial stressors and openness to injury address critical mental parts that can affect young adult emotional well-being. Stressors might incorporate scholastic tensions, cultural assumptions, family clashes, or difficulties connected with personality and confidence. The mental reaction to these stressors differs among people, for certain adolescents showing versatile adapting, while others might encounter elevated weakness to psychological well-being issues.

Horrible encounters, like physical or psychological mistreatment, disregard, or misfortune, can affect juvenile emotional well-being. The mental effect of injury might appear as side effects of post-horrendous pressure, nervousness, or sorrow. Understanding the job of psychosocial stressors and injury in molding the mental scene of youthfulness is pivotal for fitting mediations that address the extraordinary requirements of impacted people.

Mediation and Backing:

Perceiving the mental parts of juvenile psychological wellness stresses the significance of intercession and backing. Psychological wellness intercessions might incorporate directing, psychotherapy, and ability building programs that address close to home guideline, methods for dealing with hardship or stress, and flexibility. School-based emotional wellness drives, peer encouraging groups of people, and local area assets add to an extensive way to deal with juvenile psychological well-being.

Open correspondence among teens and believed grown-ups is fundamental for cultivating mental prosperity. Giving places of refuge to articulation, lessening the disgrace related with looking for help, and advancing emotional well-being training add to a strong climate for teenagers exploring the intricacies of mental difficulties. Early mediation and admittance to emotional wellness assets assume a significant part in tending to mental parts and advancing positive psychological well-being results during puberty.

2.2 Hormonal Changes and Emotional Turmoil

Hormonal Changes and Personal Unrest: Exploring the Rollercoaster of Juvenile Feelings

Immaturity, frequently inseparable from turbulent feelings and uplifted responsiveness, is unpredictably entwined with a time of huge hormonal changes. The juvenile cerebrum and body go through a mind boggling transformation, directed by the flood of chemicals that assume a significant part in forming actual turn of events, close to home prosperity, and in general emotional wellness. This investigation dives into the significant effect of hormonal changes on personal strife during youthfulness, unwinding the complex connection among science and the rollercoaster of teen feelings.

Pubescence and Hormonal Floods:

The excursion through youth starts with pubescence — an extraordinary stage described by the development of regenerative organs and the improvement of optional sexual qualities. Pubescence is organized by a fountain of hormonal changes, with the central members being sex chemicals, remembering estrogen and progesterone for females and testosterone in guys.

These hormonal floods start a progression of actual changes, for example, the development spray, improvement of bosom tissue, extending of the voice, and the beginning of monthly cycle. While these actual changes are apparent and quantifiable, it is the less substantial effect on feelings and mental prosperity that frequently characterizes the young adult experience.

Synapses and Mental health:

The impact of chemicals on personal disturbance is complicatedly connected to their effect on synapses — compound couriers in the mind that direct state of mind, feelings, and conduct. Serotonin, dopamine, and norepinephrine are synapses that assume a significant part in profound guideline, and their levels are impacted by hormonal changes during immaturity.

The limbic framework, a district of the mind related with feelings, goes through significant improvement during this period. The exchange between hormonal variances and the development of the limbic framework adds to the elevated close to home reactivity saw in youngsters. Feelings become more serious, and youths might encounter state of mind swings, crabbiness, and an increased aversion to meaningful gestures.

Personal Unrest and Hormonal Vacillations:

The connection between hormonal vacillations and personal unrest is maybe most clear in the close to home rollercoaster that numerous young people insight. The flood of sex chemicals adds to expanded profound reactivity, prompting many feelings that can change quickly and capriciously. Snapshots of euphoria might be trailed by episodes of misery or peevishness, making an unpredictable profound scene.

One remarkable perspective is the commonness of emotional episodes, which are a sign of immaturity as well as intently attached to hormonal changes. The recurring pattern of chemicals, especially estrogen and progesterone in females and testosterone in guys, add to the fluctuation of mind-sets. This close to home choppiness can be trying for the two teens and everyone around them to explore, prompting errors and uplifted relational contentions.

Influence on Pressure Reaction:

Hormonal changes during pre-adulthood additionally impact the pressure reaction framework. The nerve center pituitary-adrenal (HPA) pivot, a critical part of the pressure reaction, is regulated by chemicals like cortisol. The interaction between sex chemicals and cortisol levels influences how young people see and answer stressors.

Youths might show uplifted reactivity to stressors, and the pressure reaction framework might take more time to get back to benchmark levels. This delayed enactment of the pressure reaction can add to persistent pressure, affecting emotional well-being and possibly prompting conditions like nervousness or sorrow. Understanding the unpredictable connection between hormonal changes and the pressure reaction is essential for tending to the inner difficulties looked by teenagers.

Distinctions in sexual orientation in Hormonal Effect:

While hormonal changes are a widespread part of youthfulness, there are outstanding distinctions in sexual orientation in how these progressions manifest. In females, the period presents a repeating example of hormonal changes. The premenstrual stage, portrayed by changes in estrogen and progesterone levels, is frequently connected with temperament swings, crabbiness, and profound responsiveness.

For guys, the steady expansion in testosterone levels adds to actual changes, for example, expanded bulk and the developing of the voice. Testosterone is likewise connected to animosity and chance taking way of behaving, impacting the profound scene of young adult young men. Understanding these orientation explicit parts of hormonal effect is fundamental for fitting help and intercessions that address the interesting inner difficulties looked by the two sexes during puberty.

Relationship with Psychological wellness Issues:

The perplexing interaction between hormonal changes and personal unrest during youthfulness has suggestions for psychological wellness. The weakness made by hormonal variances might add to the beginning or intensification of psychological well-being issues. Conditions, for example, gloom and uneasiness, which frequently arise during immaturity, might be impacted by the hormonal scene.

For instance, the hormonal changes related with the monthly cycle in females might add to the improvement of premenstrual dysphoric issue (PMDD), an extreme type of premenstrual disorder portrayed by critical temperament unsettling influences. Additionally, the elevated close to home reactivity and stress reaction might add to the advancement of state of mind and nervousness problems.

It is fundamental to perceive that while hormonal changes assume a critical part in personal strife, they connect with a horde of different variables, including hereditary qualities, ecological impacts, and individual weaknesses. An exhaustive comprehension of these cooperations is urgent for tending to emotional well-being difficulties in youth.

Survival strategies and Profound Guideline:

Youths are not uninvolved beneficiaries of the hormonal changes that portray this period; they effectively participate in the advancement of survival techniques and profound guideline procedures. The capacity to explore personal strife is impacted by variables like mindfulness, social help, and the development of adapting abilities.

Solid ways of dealing with hardship or stress, like looking for social help, participating in active work, and rehearsing care, add to close to home flexibility.

Youths who foster viable profound guideline methodologies are better prepared to deal with the extreme feelings related with hormonal changes. Then again, maladaptive survival strategies, including substance use or self-hurt, may arise as endeavors to deal with inner unrest, featuring the significance of early intercession and backing.

Ecological Variables and Hormonal Collaborations:

The effect of hormonal changes on personal strife isn't segregated from ecological elements. The social setting, relational intricacies, peer connections, and cultural assumptions all associate with hormonal changes to shape the close to home encounters of young people. Ecological stressors can worsen personal disturbance, and steady conditions can moderate its effect.

The impact of innovation and virtual entertainment on young adult feelings adds one more layer to the perplexing interchange of hormonal changes and natural elements. The steady network and openness to arranged web-based personalities might add to social examination and effect confidence, affecting the close to home prosperity of youngsters.

Positive Parts of Inner Strife:

While the personal disturbance related with hormonal changes is in many cases outlined in a pessimistic light, perceiving the likely sure parts of this experience is fundamental. The elevated close to home awareness and force can add to imagination, self-revelation, and the development of profound relational associations.

Youths exploring inner disturbance might foster flexibility, sympathy, and their very own nuanced comprehension feelings. The most common way of wrestling with extreme sentiments can be groundbreaking, cultivating self-improvement and adding to the advancement of the ability to appreciate anyone on a deeper level.

Emotionally supportive networks and Mediations:

Perceiving the significant effect of hormonal changes on inner disturbance during immaturity highlights the significance of emotionally supportive networks and designated intercessions. Open correspondence among youngsters and believed grown-ups is essential for making a place of refuge for examining feelings and exploring the difficulties of pre-adulthood.

School-based psychological well-being drives, peer encouraging groups of people, and local area assets assume an essential part in furnishing teenagers with the devices and survival strategies expected to explore personal strife. Psychological well-being schooling that incorporates data about the natural underpinnings of close to home encounters can add to expanded mindfulness and lessen shame around examining emotional wellness.

Early intercession and admittance to psychological well-being assets are fundamental for tending to psychological well-being difficulties related with hormonal changes. Psychological wellness experts can work cooperatively with young people to foster survival techniques, upgrade close to home guideline abilities, and give a steady system to exploring the intricacies of feelings during this basic formative period.

2.3 Peer Pressure and Social Dynamics

Peer Tension and Social Elements: Exploring the Effect on Juvenile Turn of events

The complicated embroidery of pre-adulthood is woven with hormonal changes as well as with the strong impact of companion strain and social elements. The craving for social acknowledgment, the need to have a place, and the steady assessment by peers shape the encounters of young people, adding to both positive and testing parts of their turn of events. This investigation digs into the multi-layered elements of friend strain and social elements, disentangling the intricacies of how associations with peers impact the direction of young adult turn of events.

The Meaning of Companion Connections:

Peer connections possess a focal job in the social and close to home scene of puberty. As teens endeavor to lay out their characters, explore cultural assumptions, and fashion a feeling of having a place, peer connections become an essential wellspring of impact. The meaning of friend connections stretches out past simple friendship; they act as a mirror reflecting cultural standards, values, and assumptions.

During immaturity, there is a characteristic tendency for people to look for independence from their families and investigate associations with peers. This change in center from family to peers is a formative achievement, denoting the development of freedom and the development of a social character. Peer connections give a stage to self-disclosure, shared encounters, and the improvement of interactive abilities pivotal for exploring the more extensive social scene.

Positive Parts of Friend Impact:

Peer impact isn't intrinsically regrettable; it envelops both positive and valuable aspects. Positive parts of companion impact during youth incorporate the improvement of interactive abilities, the development of sympathy, and the arrangement of enduring fellowships. As teens cooperate with different people, they figure out how to explore social subtleties, convey actually, and grasp the viewpoints of others.

Peer connections likewise offer basic reassurance and a feeling of having a place. Kinships framed during immaturity add to the close to home prosperity of people, offering a help framework to explore the difficulties of this formative stage. Positive friend impact cultivates a feeling of kinship, shared values, and the chance for common development as people explore the excursion of self-revelation together.

Difficulties of Negative Companion Tension:

While positive companion impact is essential to solid juvenile turn of events, the apparition of negative friend pressure poses a potential threat. The craving to fit in, keep away from dismissal, and adjust to apparent normal practices can lead young people to settle on decisions that are not lined up with their qualities or helpful for their prosperity. Negative companion pressure appears in ways of behaving, for example, substance use, dangerous ways of behaving, and commitment to exercises that might think twice about or emotional wellness.

The effect of negative companion pressure is exacerbated by the uplifted weakness of youngsters to outer impacts. The as yet creating prefrontal cortex — the locale liable for independent direction and drive control — may add to a defenselessness to surrender to peer strain without completely thinking about the results. The interaction between the requirement for social acknowledgment and the potential for adverse impact makes a fragile equilibrium that shapes the conduct selections of youths.

Social Examination and Its Suggestions:

Social examination, a characteristic mental cycle, assumes a urgent part in the elements of friend impact. Youths frequently participate in friendly correlation, considering themselves in contrast to their companions in different spaces, including scholastics, appearance, and societal position. While social examination can act as an inspiration for personal growth, it likewise conveys the gamble of encouraging insecurities, low confidence, and the quest for ridiculous principles.

The unavoidable impact of web-based entertainment intensifies the effect of social correlation, establishing a climate where organized internet based characters and virtual collaborations add to a twisted feeling of the real world. The strain to adjust to these glorified pictures can prompt the assimilation of unreasonable excellence guidelines, scholarly assumptions, and way of life decisions, further energizing negative companion impact.

Personality Development and Congruity:

The course of personality development during immaturity is unpredictably connected with the elements of congruity inside peer gatherings. Youths might encounter a pressure between the craving to communicate their distinction and the need to adjust to the standards of their friend bunch. The apprehension about dismissal and the journey for social acknowledgment can prompt similarity, where people take on ways of behaving, convictions, or perspectives that line up with those of their friends.

Congruity inside peer gatherings might impact different parts of juvenile life, including style decisions, language use, and support in specific exercises. While congruity is a characteristic piece of socialization, extreme similarity that compromises bona fide self-articulation can negatively affect individual personality improvement.

Finding some kind of harmony between finding a place with peers and keeping a feeling of singularity is a sensitive test looked by youths.

Influence on Scholarly Execution:

Peer tension can apply a huge effect on scholarly execution during puberty. The impact of friend standards, concentrate on propensities, and mentalities toward training can shape the scholarly decisions and accomplishments of youngsters. Positive companion impact in scholarly settings might encourage a culture of tirelessness, inspiration, and cooperative learning.

On the other hand, negative companion strain can prompt withdrawal from scholarly pursuits, the prioritization of social exercises over homework, and a hesitance to look for scholastic help. The feeling of dread toward being seen as scholastically fruitless or 'ho hum' may add to a hesitance to participate in advancing completely. The scholarly results of negative friend pressure feature the requirement for a steady scholastic climate that empowers positive companion impact and a pledge to instructive achievement.

Versatility and Survival strategies:

The capacity of youths to explore the difficulties of companion strain and social elements is intently attached to their flexibility and methods for dealing with stress. Strong people have the ability to endure pessimistic impacts, return from misfortunes, and keep a healthy identity viability. The improvement of versatility is impacted by variables like areas of strength for an of self, steady associations with grown-ups, and the development of adapting abilities.

Sound survival strategies assume a significant part in moderating the effect of negative companion pressure. Young people outfitted with successful survival methods, for example, critical thinking abilities, profound guideline procedures, and decisiveness, are better situated to oppose pessimistic impacts and pursue decisions lined up with their qualities. Intercessions that attention on upgrading versatility and showing versatile strategies for dealing with stress add to the general prosperity of young people confronting peer-related difficulties.

Parental Impact and Correspondence:

The job of guardians in forming the reaction of young people to peer pressure couldn't possibly be more significant. Positive parent-kid connections portrayed by open correspondence, trust, and backing make an establishment for strength. At the point when teens have a good sense of safety in their associations with guardians, they are bound to look for direction, share concerns, and oppose negative friend impacts.

Successful correspondence among guardians and young people includes undivided attention, sympathy, and the arrangement of direction without judgment. Parental association in the public activities of teens, including consciousness of friend connections and exercises, empowers guardians to offer help and direction in exploring the intricacies of companion pressure.

Parental impact fills in as an offset to peer impact, adding to the improvement of a solid sense of direction in teenagers.

School-Based Intercessions and Companion Encouraging groups of people:

Schools assume a significant part in tending to the difficulties presented by peer strain and encouraging positive social elements. School-based mediations might incorporate projects that advance social and close to home learning, versatility building studios, and hostile to harassing drives. Peer encouraging groups of people and tutoring programs set out open doors for positive companion impact and the improvement of a steady school local area.

Instructive educational plans that integrate points connected with peer pressure, media proficiency, and the effect of social elements on emotional wellness add to the general prosperity of understudies. By furnishing young people with the information and abilities to explore peer-related difficulties, schools assume a crucial part in forming a positive and comprehensive social climate.

2.4 Academic Stressors and Expectations

Scholarly Stressors and Assumptions: Unwinding the Complicated Embroidery of Adolescent Scholastic Life

Immaturity, set apart by the turbulent excursion through secondary school and the quest for scholarly greatness, is much of the time portrayed by a snare of scholastic stressors and assumptions. The strain to succeed, explore complex instructive scenes, and live up to cultural assumptions makes a one of a kind arrangement of difficulties for youngsters. This investigation digs into the diverse components of scholastic stressors and assumptions, disentangling the many-sided woven artwork that shapes the scholarly existences of adolescents.

The Heaviness of Assumptions:

As teenagers progress from center school to secondary school, the heaviness of scholarly assumptions strengthens. The cultural accentuation on scholastic achievement, school readiness, and future profession possibilities puts an extensive weight on youngsters. Assumptions radiate from different sources, including guardians, educators, peers, and the more extensive cultural story that frequently likens scholarly accomplishment with future achievement.

Guardians, in their yearnings for their youngsters, may hold onto elevated standards, imagining a direction of scholarly achievement that lines up with cultural standards. Educators, entrusted with planning understudies for the difficulties of advanced education and the labor force, may incidentally add to the strain by setting thorough principles. Peer examinations further enhance the feeling of assumption, as young people measure their scholastic accomplishments against those of their schoolmates.

High-Stakes Testing and Scholastic Execution:

The scene of scholastic stressors is interspersed by high-stakes testing, a foundation of the schooling system in numerous locales. Government sanctioned tests, school placement tests, and other evaluative evaluations establish a climate where scholastic execution is compared with an understudy's worth and potential for future achievement. The strain to succeed in these evaluations can turn into a huge wellspring of stress for youngsters.

High-stakes testing acquaints a serious component with scholarly pursuits, encouraging a culture where achievement is estimated by mathematical scores and percentile rankings. The apprehension about failing to meet expectations, not measuring up to assumptions, or imperiling future open doors heightens the pressure related with scholastic accomplishment. The ramifications of these appraisals on school confirmations further increase the stakes, adding to the general weight on understudies.

Extracurricular Requests and Using time productively:

The quest for scholarly greatness frequently interlaces with extracurricular exercises, adding one more layer of intricacy to the high school insight. While contribution in extracurriculars is supported for all encompassing turn of events, it likewise presents extra requests on an understudy's significant investment. Offsetting scholarly obligations with the responsibilities of clubs, sports, or creative pursuits turns into a shuffling act that calls for compelling using time effectively.

The craving to fabricate a powerful school application, exhibit balance, and develop a different range of abilities can lead youngsters to extend themselves slight. The strain to succeed scholastically while effectively taking part in extracurriculars requires a fragile equilibrium, and the feeling of dread toward missing the mark in either domain adds to the general stressors experienced by youths.

Progress to Advanced education and Vocation Yearnings:

As teens approach the zenith of their secondary school venture, the approaching progress to advanced education or the labor force adds one more layer of scholarly pressure. The assumptions encompassing school confirmations, grant valuable open doors, and the arrangement of scholarly decisions with future profession yearnings make a need to get a move on and vulnerability. The strain to come to urgent conclusions around one's instructive and proficient direction turns into a critical part of scholastic stressors.

The serious idea of school confirmations, combined with the apparent significance of choosing the "right" major or vocation way, enhances the pressure related with these choices. Young people might wrestle with the feeling of dread toward settling on some unacceptable decisions that could influence their future achievement and satisfaction.

The accentuation on a straight and distinct way further adds to the heaviness of scholastic assumptions during this momentary stage.

Influence on Psychological wellness:

The aggregate impact of scholarly stressors and assumptions has significant ramifications for the emotional well-being of teens. Young people might encounter side effects of pressure, tension, and even melancholy as they explore the unpredictable scene of scholarly tensions. The apprehension about disappointment, the persistent quest for flawlessness, and the staggering requests on their significant investment add to the disintegration of mental prosperity.

The strain to measure up to scholarly assumptions can appear in different ways, including rest aggravations, changes in craving, and trouble concentrating. Elevated degrees of stress might prompt burnout, influencing scholarly execution as well as generally wellbeing and personal satisfaction. Tending to the psychological wellness ramifications of scholarly pressure requires an all encompassing methodology that recognizes the interconnectedness of scholastic, profound, and actual prosperity.

Parental Assumptions and Correspondence:

The job of guardians in forming scholastic assumptions and it is crucial to moderate pressure. While parental yearnings for their youngsters' prosperity are regular and good natured, finding some kind of harmony that encourages a solid scholarly environment is fundamental. Open correspondence among guardians and youngsters, portrayed by undivided attention, sympathy, and an emphasis on seeing as opposed to forcing assumptions, adds to a steady familial setting.

Guardians can assume a key part in easing scholastic pressure by cultivating practical assumptions, empowering a development outlook, and stressing the significance of exertion as opposed to exclusively result. Perceiving and praising a youngster's singular assets and achievements, independent of outside benchmarks, adds to a positive scholastic outlook.

Schooling System Changes and Prosperity Drives:

The construction of the schooling system itself assumes a critical part in molding scholastic stressors. Calls for changes that focus on comprehensive instruction, de-underline inordinate state sanctioned testing, and advance a different scope of abilities and gifts have built up momentum. Such changes intend to establish an instructive climate that sustains inventiveness, decisive reasoning, and individualized learning, instead of exclusively zeroing in on repetition remembrance and test execution.

Notwithstanding foundational changes, drives inside schools to focus on understudy prosperity are acquiring significance. Psychological wellness support administrations, directing projects, and stress decrease exercises add to a more adjusted instructive experience. Making a culture that values prosperity close by scholarly accomplishment is fundamental for cultivating versatility and forestalling the adverse consequence of scholastic stressors on understudies.

Showing Methodologies and Understudy Driven Approaches:

Teachers assume a critical part in moderating scholastic stressors by embracing instructing techniques that focus on grasping over remembrance, empower cooperation, and consider different learning styles. Understudy driven approaches that perceive individual qualities and give open doors to independent learning add to a positive scholastic climate.

Encouraging a development mentality — the conviction that capacities and knowledge can be created through commitment and difficult work — makes an establishment for flexibility notwithstanding scholastic difficulties. Teachers can effectively advance a development outlook by lauding exertion, giving useful input, and stressing the growing experience as opposed to zeroing in exclusively on grades and execution results.

Peer Encouraging groups of people and Cooperation:
Peer connections, while adding to social correlation and possible adverse impacts, likewise offer the chance for positive joint effort and backing. Peer encouraging groups of people can assume a huge part in assisting teens with exploring scholastic stressors. Cooperative learning conditions, concentrate on gatherings, and mentorship programs give roads to shared encounters, common support, and the advancement of successful review techniques.

Advancing a culture of scholarly joint effort over undesirable contest encourages a climate where understudies can uphold each other's prosperity. Peer tutoring drives, where more established understudies guide more youthful ones through scholarly difficulties, add to a feeling of local area and shared liability regarding scholastic prosperity.

Chapter 3

The Interplay of Teen Angst and Ortho Hurdles

The Interaction of High schooler Apprehension and Muscular Obstacles: Exploring the Physical and Profound Scene of Puberty

Youthfulness, a period set apart by both physical and personal disturbances, delivers a mind boggling transaction of youngster tension and muscular obstacles. The excursion through these early stages isn't just described by the difficulties of exploring personality, connections, and scholarly tensions yet additionally by the actual changes and muscular issues that can essentially affect the general prosperity of youngsters. This investigation digs into the many-sided connection between adolescent tension and muscular obstacles, disentangling the physical and close to home scene of pre-adulthood.

Actual Development and Muscular Difficulties:

The young adult years are inseparable from quick actual development and advancement. As teens go through development sprays, the skeletal framework goes through significant changes, with bones extending and joints adjusting to the requests of the creating body.

While this time of development is fundamental for accomplishing grown-up height, it likewise presents the potential for muscular difficulties.

One pervasive muscular issue during puberty is developing torments. These are regularly described by limited uneasiness or hurting in the muscles and bones, especially in the legs. Developing torments are much of the time a consequence of the lopsided pace of development among bones and muscles, prompting impermanent inconvenience. While they are viewed as an ordinary piece of development, developing torments can add to a feeling of actual disquiet and distress, adding to the general difficulties of pre-adulthood.

Sports Wounds and Actual work:

The quest for proactive tasks and commitment to sports is a typical part of juvenile life. While support in sports brings various physical and psychological well-being benefits, it likewise opens youngsters to the gamble of sports-related wounds. Muscular wounds, like injuries, strains, cracks, and abuse wounds, can happen because of serious actual work and ill-advised preparing methods.

Sports wounds act actual difficulties like well as have mental ramifications. Teenagers energetic about sports might encounter dissatisfaction, frustration, and a feeling of misfortune when sidelined because of wounds. The transaction between the craving to succeed in actual pursuits and the need to explore muscular obstacles adds to the complex close to home scene of youngster competitors.

Stance, Ergonomics, and Outer muscle Wellbeing:

The predominance of stationary ways of behaving, including delayed times of screen time and work area bound exercises, adds one more aspect to the interchange of high schooler anxiety and muscular obstacles. Unfortunate stance, deficient ergonomics, and delayed sitting add to outer muscle issues, including back torment, neck agony, and unfortunate spinal arrangement.

The actual distress related with outer muscle issues can affect profound prosperity. Constant agony or inconvenience might prompt crabbiness, trouble concentrating, and in general disappointment. The need to address muscular worries, advance legitimate stance, and underscore outer muscle wellbeing becomes essential in supporting both the physical and close to home components of juvenile turn of events.

Self-perception, Self-Discernment, and Muscular Circumstances:

Muscular circumstances, like scoliosis or appendage length disparities, can impact self-perception and self-discernment during pre-adulthood. The longing for similarity with cultural guidelines of actual appearance might be uplifted during this formative stage, and muscular issues that go astray from apparent standards might add to reluctance and close to home pain.

Scoliosis, portrayed by a sidelong bend of the spine, is one muscular condition that can influence self-perception. Teenagers with scoliosis might encounter worries about the balance of their body and expected perceivability of the condition. While headways in muscular medicines offer mediations for conditions like scoliosis, tending to the profound parts of self-perception during muscular difficulties is fundamental for all encompassing prosperity.

Persistent Muscular Circumstances and Emotional well-being:

A few youths face persistent muscular circumstances, like adolescent idiopathic joint inflammation or osteogenesis imperfecta, which require progressing the board and may present difficulties to physical and close to home prosperity. Constant agony, restrictions in portability, and the requirement for clinical mediations can add to uplifted feelings of anxiety and close to home battles.

The close to home effect of persistent muscular circumstances might appear in nervousness, wretchedness, or sensations of detachment. Young people managing these difficulties might wrestle with inquiries of self-personality and acknowledgment. A strong multidisciplinary approach that tends to both the physical and close to home parts of constant muscular circumstances is fundamental for cultivating strength and positive emotional well-being results.

Muscular Intercessions and Close to home Strength:

Muscular mediations, including medical procedures, active recuperation, and orthotic gadgets, are normal ways to deal with address muscular obstacles in youths. While these mediations plan to work on actual capability and relieve torment, they likewise require a level of close to home versatility from young people. The most common way of going through muscular medicines might bring out uneasiness, dread, or worries about self-perception.

Preoperative training, open correspondence between medical care suppliers and youths, and mental help assume significant parts in planning young people for muscular mediations. Engaging teenagers with data about their condition and including them in dynamic cycles encourages a feeling of organization and adds to close to home strength during muscular medicines.

Peer Connections, Social Elements, and Muscular Difficulties:

The effect of muscular difficulties stretches out to social elements and friend connections during pre-adulthood. Young people might confront difficulties connected with social consideration, as muscular circumstances might impact proactive tasks and support in specific get-togethers. The longing to fit in and try not to be seen as various may add to profound pressure for youths managing muscular obstacles.

Peer backing and positive social elements are pivotal for the close to home prosperity of youngsters confronting muscular difficulties. Comprehensive conditions that advance sympathy, understanding, and acknowledgment add to a strong social scene. Instructing peers about muscular circumstances, cultivating a culture of inclusivity, and empowering open correspondence lessen the potential for social disconnection and upgrade the generally speaking profound flexibility of teenagers with muscular obstacles.

Parental Help and Correspondence:

The job of guardians in offering help and cultivating open correspondence is principal for youths exploring muscular difficulties. Guardians act as backers for their teens, guaranteeing admittance to suitable medical care, muscular mediations, and daily reassurance. Open conversations about muscular circumstances, treatment choices, and potential difficulties make an establishment for understanding and acknowledgment inside the family.

Underlining the significance of generally prosperity, including physical and profound aspects, adds to an all encompassing way to deal with muscular obstacles. Guardians assume an essential part in imparting a positive mentality, advancing strength, and working with the improvement of survival techniques that engage youths to explore both the physical and profound parts of muscular difficulties.

Joining of Psychological well-being and Muscular Consideration:

Perceiving the interconnectedness of psychological wellness and muscular consideration is fundamental for offering extensive help to young people. Coordinated care models that include cooperation between muscular subject matter experts and psychological well-being experts guarantee a comprehensive way to deal with treatment. This coordinated effort tends to the actual side effects as well as the close to home and mental parts of muscular difficulties.

Psychosocial evaluations, directing administrations, and psychological wellness intercessions supplement muscular consideration, adding to a more exhaustive and patient-focused approach. This coordinated model recognizes the effect of profound prosperity on the general recuperation and versatility of teenagers managing muscular obstacles.

Instructive and Mindfulness Drives:

Instructive drives pointed toward bringing issues to light about muscular circumstances, their effect on youths, and accessible assets add to a more educated and compassionate society. Schools assume a fundamental part in establishing comprehensive conditions that advance comprehension and lessen disgrace connected with muscular difficulties.

Integrating muscular wellbeing training into school educational programs encourages a culture of acknowledgment and backing. Mindfulness drives that feature the encounters of youths with muscular circumstances, their accomplishments, and commitments to society add to changing discernments and diminishing cultural obstructions.

3.1 Linking Emotional Well-being to Physical Health

Connecting Profound Prosperity to Actual Wellbeing: The Indivisible Congruity of Brain and Body

The complicated dance between profound prosperity and actual wellbeing structures the underpinning of an all encompassing way to deal with in general health. Lately, there has been a change in outlook in perceiving the significant interconnection among mental and actual wellbeing. This investigation digs into the complex embroidery that joins close to home prosperity to actual wellbeing, disentangling the harmonious relationship that shapes the general wellbeing and versatility of people.

The Psyche Body Association:

The idea of the psyche body association highlights the indispensable connection among mental and actual prosperity. A long way from working in confinement, the brain and body participate in steady correspondence, each impacting and forming the other. This bidirectional correspondence happens through complex pathways including the sensory system, hormonal reactions, and resistant capabilities, making a unique interaction that essentially influences wellbeing results.

Feelings, whether good or pessimistic, include physiological appearances inside the body. The experience of happiness might set off the arrival of synapses like dopamine and endorphins, adding to a feeling of prosperity. On the other hand, stress or tension can enact the body's pressure reaction, delivering cortisol and adrenaline, which, if constant, may prompt a scope of actual medical problems. Perceiving and understanding this perplexing dance among feelings and actual reactions is urgent for cultivating an exhaustive way to deal with wellbeing.

Influence on Cardiovascular Wellbeing:

The impact of close to home prosperity on cardiovascular wellbeing is especially critical. Ongoing pressure, portrayed by delayed actuation of the body's pressure reaction framework, is connected to an expanded gamble of cardiovascular illnesses. The consistent arrival of stress chemicals can add to raised circulatory strain, aggravation, and changes in vein capability, which are all critical gamble factors for heart-related issues.

On the other hand, positive close to home prosperity, including encounters of satisfaction, bliss, and social connectedness, has been related with better cardiovascular results. Participating in exercises that advance profound strength, like care, contemplation, and positive social communications, adds to the upkeep of cardiovascular wellbeing. The significant effect of profound states on the cardiovascular framework highlights the requirement for intercessions that address both close to home prosperity and actual wellbeing.

The Insusceptible Framework and Mental Pressure:

The safe framework, a mind boggling organization of cells and proteins that guards the body against contaminations and illnesses, is complicatedly associated with close to home prosperity. Mental pressure, if ongoing or extreme, can smother resistant capability, making people more helpless to contaminations and weakening the body's capacity to mount a powerful invulnerable reaction.

On the other hand, positive feelings and a feeling of prosperity have been related with upgraded invulnerable capability. The arrival of neuropeptides and other insusceptible controlling particles during positive close to home states might add to the fortifying of the invulnerable framework. This association accentuates the job of profound wellbeing in supporting the body's guard systems and by and large strength against ailments.

Hormonal Guideline and Close to home States:

The endocrine framework, liable for creating and controlling chemicals, is a central member in the convergence of profound prosperity and actual wellbeing. Chemicals, for example, cortisol, assume a vital part in the body's reaction to push. Persistent pressure can disturb the typical working of the endocrine framework, prompting uneven characters in chemical levels that add to a scope of medical problems, including metabolic issues and resistant concealment.

The hypothalamic-pituitary-adrenal (HPA) pivot, a focal part of the pressure reaction framework, is firmly connected to close to home states. Close to home stressors can initiate the HPA pivot, prompting the arrival of cortisol. While intense initiation of this framework is an ordinary reaction to stretch, constant enactment can add to a condition of allostatic load — a condition where the body's administrative frameworks are exhausted, prompting mileage on different physiological frameworks.

Gastrointestinal Wellbeing and the Stomach Mind Hub:

The stomach cerebrum hub, a bidirectional correspondence framework between the gastrointestinal plot and the mind, features the association between close to home prosperity and gastrointestinal wellbeing. Profound states, especially stress and uneasiness, can affect the capability of the gastrointestinal framework, prompting side effects like heartburn, touchy gut condition (IBS), and changes in stomach motility.

On the other hand, the strength of the stomach microbiome, the local area of microorganisms in the gastrointestinal system, has been connected to psychological wellness results. The stomach microbiome produces synapses and speaks with the focal sensory system, impacting mind-set and profound states. Awkward nature in the stomach microbiome, frequently connected with unfortunate dietary decisions, can add to both gastrointestinal issues and psychological wellness challenges.

Persistent Agony and Mental Prosperity:

Persistent torment, a complex and frequently crippling condition, embodies the perplexing connection between actual side effects and profound prosperity. The experience of tenacious agony can prompt close to home pain, including sensations of disappointment, uneasiness, and sorrow. On the other hand, profound states can adjust the impression of agony, impacting torment edges and the general insight of distress.

The bidirectional connection between ongoing torment and mental prosperity features the significance of tending to the two viewpoints in an extensive treatment approach. Integrative agony the board methodologies that consolidate actual intercessions with mental help, for example, mental social treatment and care, expect to address the complex idea of persistent agony.

Brain adaptability and Close to home Strength:

Brain adaptability, the mind's capacity to adjust and redesign itself in light of encounters and natural improvements, assumes a vital part in the exchange between profound prosperity and actual wellbeing. Constant pressure and pessimistic close to home states can impact the design and capability of the cerebrum, adding to changes in brain circuits related with mind-set guideline and stress reaction.

On the other hand, rehearses that advance profound flexibility and positive prosperity, like contemplation and mental conduct mediations, have been related with positive changes in mind construction and capability. These changes, driven by brain adaptability, highlight the potential for intercessions that upgrade close to home strength to influence both mental and actual wellbeing results decidedly.

The Effect of Social Associations:

Social associations, a foundation of close to home prosperity, apply a significant impact on actual wellbeing. Solid social encouraging groups of people have been connected to better wellbeing results, including lower paces of persistent illnesses, worked on insusceptible capability, and expanded life span. In actuality, social confinement and sensations of depression are related with unfriendly wellbeing impacts, including uplifted pressure reactions, cardiovascular issues, and compromised resistant capability.

The nature of social cooperations, the profundity of relational connections, and the feeling of having a place inside a local area add to the effect of social associations on wellbeing. Perceiving the meaning of social prosperity in the general wellbeing condition stresses the requirement for mediations that cultivate local area, diminish social seclusion, and advance positive social communications.

Strength and Survival techniques:

The capacity to explore life's difficulties with strength and compelling survival strategies is a key part in the connection between close to home prosperity and actual wellbeing. Versatile people show flexibility notwithstanding difficulty, keep an uplifting perspective, and really adapt to stressors. The development of flexibility contributes not exclusively to close to home prosperity yet in addition to the relief of the physiological impacts of ongoing pressure.

Powerful survival techniques, for example, critical thinking abilities, social help usage, and care rehearses, assume a urgent part in dealing with profound states and advancing generally wellbeing. Intercessions that emphasis on upgrading adapting abilities add to a complete procedure for tending to the interweaved idea of profound prosperity and actual wellbeing.

Preventive and Integrative Methodologies:

A preventive and integrative way to deal with wellbeing perceives the indivisible idea of close to home prosperity and actual wellbeing. Preventive procedures that include psychological wellness screenings, stress the executives projects, and wellbeing training add to early ID and intercession for people in danger of encountering pessimistic wellbeing results.

Integrative medical services models, which join conventional clinical mediations with correlative methodologies, recognize the multi-faceted parts of wellbeing. Integrative practices like yoga, needle therapy, and reflection offer actual medical advantages as well as address profound prosperity, making a synergistic methodology that advances generally health.

3.2 Impact of Stress on Ortho Conditions

The Interlaced Strings: Investigating the Effect of Weight on Muscular Circumstances

The unpredictable exchange among pressure and muscular circumstances discloses a convincing story where the domains of mental and actual prosperity combine. Stress, a pervasive part of present day life, can project significant waves that reach out past the domain of feelings to impact muscular wellbeing unpredictably. This investigation dives into the multi-layered elements of stress and its effect on muscular circumstances, disentangling the complex web that ties the brain and body with regards to outer muscle wellbeing.

The Pressure Ortho Association:

The association among stress and muscular circumstances lives in the perplexing connection between the sensory system, outer muscle framework, and the body's reaction to stressors. Stress sets off a fountain of physiological reactions, including the arrival of stress chemicals, for example, cortisol and adrenaline, which can apply an immediate effect on the outer muscle framework.

Persistent pressure, portrayed by delayed openness to stressors without satisfactory unwinding or recuperation, can add to the turn of events or fuel of muscular circumstances. The effect of weight on the body's fiery reaction, resistant capability, and muscle pressure assumes a urgent part in forming the scene of outer muscle wellbeing.

Fiery Reaction and Joint Wellbeing:

The body's fiery reaction, regularly a defensive system in light of injury or contamination, can be impacted by persistent pressure. Delayed pressure might prompt an overactive fiery reaction, adding to constant irritation — a sign of different muscular circumstances.

With regards to joints, persistent irritation can assume a part in the movement of conditions like rheumatoid joint inflammation and osteoarthritis. In rheumatoid joint pain, an immune system condition, stress might possibly fuel the fiery cycle, prompting expanded joint agony and firmness. In osteoarthritis, the mileage of joints might be impacted by irritation, with stress going about as a potential modulator of this fiery reaction.

Muscle Strain and Stress-incited Agony:

Muscle strain, a typical physiological reaction to push, can add to the indication of stress-prompted torment and muscular inconvenience. At the point when the body is under pressure, muscles may automatically contract and fix, prompting an uplifted condition of strain. Delayed muscle strain can add to the improvement of conditions like pressure migraines, temporomandibular joint (TMJ) messes, and myofascial torment disorders.

With regards to the spine, stress-prompted muscle strain might assume a part in the turn of events or fuel of conditions, for example, neck torment and low back torment. People with elevated degrees of stress may unknowingly embrace unfortunate stances or participate in redundant developments that add to outer muscle strain, possibly prompting persistent agony conditions.

Influence on Bone Wellbeing and Recuperating:

Stress can apply a nuanced impact on bone wellbeing, influencing both the thickness and mending cycles of bones. Constant pressure might add to diminished bone thickness, possibly expanding the gamble of conditions like osteoporosis. The unpredictable connection between stress, hormonal irregular characteristics, (for example, raised cortisol levels), and bone digestion highlights the significance of tending to pressure as an expected calculate bone wellbeing.

Also, the mending cycles of bones can be impacted by pressure. People going through muscular methodology or recuperating from breaks might encounter more slow mending or inconveniences assuming feelings of anxiety are high. Stress-actuated changes in blood stream, safe capability, and hormonal equilibrium can affect the body's capacity to fix and recover bone tissue effectively.

Muscular Circumstances as Stressors:

The connection among stress and muscular circumstances isn't unidirectional — muscular circumstances themselves can become stressors, adding to a pattern of actual uneasiness and profound pain. Constant torment, restricted portability, and the difficulties related with overseeing muscular circumstances can prompt pressure and adversely influence mental prosperity.

For people living with conditions like persistent back agony, joint pain, or outer muscle wounds, the day to day weight of overseeing side effects and exploring the restrictions forced by muscular circumstances can add to elevated feelings of anxiety. This repetitive relationship highlights the requirement for a comprehensive way to deal with care that tends to both the physical and close to home components of muscular wellbeing.

Psychosocial Variables in Muscular Recuperation:

The psychosocial parts of a singular's life, including stressors, for example, business related pressures, relational peculiarities, and financial variables, assume a vital part in muscular recuperation. Stressors outside the domain of the outer muscle framework can affect a singular's capacity to participate in recovery, stick to treatment plans, and adapt to the difficulties of muscular circumstances.

For instance, work related pressure might block a singular's capacity to enjoy vital reprieves or change their workplace to oblige muscular worries. Monetary stressors might restrict admittance to essential medicines or restoration administrations. The acknowledgment of psychosocial factors as fundamental parts of muscular consideration stresses the requirement for an exhaustive methodology that thinks about the more extensive setting of a singular's life.

Social Reactions to Stress and Muscular Wellbeing:

People answer pressure in different ways, and these conduct reactions can have suggestions for muscular wellbeing. Stress-actuated ways of behaving like indulging, inactive propensities, or the utilization of substances like tobacco and liquor might add to the turn of events or worsening of muscular circumstances.

Unfortunate survival techniques, for example, staying away from active work because of stress or utilizing substances to adapt to profound misery, can influence outer muscle wellbeing. Inactive ways of life related with constant pressure might add to weight gain and corpulence, the two of which are risk factors for muscular circumstances like osteoarthritis and joint agony.

The Job of Pressure The executives in Muscular Consideration:

Perceiving the effect of weight on muscular wellbeing features the significance of incorporating pressure the executives techniques into muscular consideration plans.

Stress decrease strategies, for example, care, unwinding works out, and mental social mediations, can supplement conventional muscular medicines to address both the physical and close to home elements of outer muscle wellbeing.

Integrating pressure the board into recovery programs for muscular circumstances improves in general prosperity and may add to better treatment results. All encompassing muscular consideration that considers the interconnected idea of stress and outer muscle wellbeing is fundamental for advancing long haul recuperation and forestalling the repeat of muscular issues.

Patient Training and Strengthening:

Teaching people about the pressure muscular association is a significant part of engaging patients to take part in their muscular consideration effectively. Giving data about the effect of weight on outer muscle wellbeing, as well as offering pressure the board assets, furnishes people with the information and apparatuses to oversee both the physical and profound parts of their circumstances.

Enabling patients to perceive and address stressors in their lives encourages a feeling of organization and self-viability. By coordinating pressure the board into the generally speaking muscular consideration plan, medical services suppliers can add to a more exhaustive and patient-focused approach that perceives the interconnected idea of stress and outer muscle prosperity.

3.3 Behavioral Factors in Orthopedic Health

Social Variables in Muscular Wellbeing: Exploring the Crossing point of Way of life and Outer muscle Prosperity

The scene of muscular wellbeing is unpredictably formed by a bunch of conduct factors that stretch out past the bounds of simple life structures and physiology. Way of life decisions, propensities, and day to day ways of behaving contribute fundamentally to the turn of events, movement, and the board of muscular circumstances. This investigation digs into the multi-layered elements of social variables in muscular wellbeing, disentangling the perplexing transaction between way of life decisions and outer muscle prosperity.

Actual work and Muscular Wellbeing:

At the center of muscular wellbeing lies the significant effect of actual work. Ordinary activity, enveloping both cardiovascular and strength preparing parts, assumes a critical part in keeping up with the honesty of the outer muscle framework. Weight-bearing activities add to bone thickness, while fortifying activities upgrade the strength and capability of muscles and joints.

On the other hand, a stationary way of life represents a huge gamble to muscular wellbeing. Delayed times of sitting or latency can add to muscle lopsided characteristics, joint firmness, and an elevated gamble of muscular circumstances like osteoarthritis. The job of actual work stretches out past counteraction, as it likewise shapes a foundation of recovery for people overseeing muscular issues.

Stance and Ergonomics:

How people convey themselves, both in static and dynamic exercises, altogether impacts muscular wellbeing. Appropriate stance is principal for keeping up with the normal arrangement of the spine and supporting the designs of the outer muscle framework. Unfortunate stance, whether during sitting, standing, or taking part in exercises, can add to outer muscle uneven characters and increment the gamble of conditions, for example, back agony and neck strain.

Ergonomics, the study of planning and orchestrating conditions to upgrade human prosperity, is especially important with regards to muscular wellbeing. Legitimate ergonomics in the work environment, home, and sporting settings can alleviate the effect of tedious strain and diminish the gamble of muscular issues connected with unfortunate stance.

Sustenance and Bone Wellbeing:

Nourishment assumes a vital part in supporting the wellbeing of bones and joints. Sufficient admission of fundamental supplements, including calcium, vitamin D, and different micronutrients, is urgent for keeping up with bone thickness and supporting the renovating system. Calcium, specifically, is essential to bone wellbeing, and an inadequacy can add to conditions like osteoporosis.

On the other hand, unfortunate nourishment can think twice about wellbeing. Awkward nature in diet, including unreasonable utilization of handled food varieties, sweet drinks, and deficient admission of fundamental supplements, may add to irritation and effect the body's capacity to fix and recover outer muscle tissues. Individuals wholesome decisions have extensive ramifications for their muscular prosperity.

Body Weight and Muscular Effect:

The connection between body weight and muscular wellbeing is a unique interchange with critical ramifications. Abundance body weight puts expanded weight on the joints, especially those of the lower furthest points. Conditions, for example, osteoarthritis, particularly in weight-bearing joints like the knees and hips, are more common among people with stoutness.

Weight the board turns into a basic part of muscular consideration, both for forestalling the beginning of outer muscle conditions and overseeing existing issues. Solid weight support lessens the heap on joints, lightens strain on the spine, and adds to generally muscular wellbeing.

Footwear and Muscular Help:

The decision of footwear is a conduct factor that frequently goes underrated in its effect on muscular wellbeing. Sick fitting shoes, inappropriate curve support, and lacking shock ingestion can add to foot issues, lower leg shakiness, and even reach out to influence the arrangement of the spine.

Alternately, legitimate footwear that offers sufficient help and padding can add to the avoidance and the board of muscular issues. People with explicit foot conditions or concerns might profit from orthotic embeds or redid footwear to address their extraordinary requirements. The thought of footwear as a conduct factor highlights the all encompassing methodology expected for far reaching muscular consideration.

Smoking and Outer muscle Wellbeing:

The social variable of smoking has extensive ramifications for outer muscle wellbeing. Smoking has been connected to diminished bone thickness, postponed break mending, and an expanded gamble of complexities after muscular medical procedures. The impeding impacts of smoking on blood stream and oxygen conveyance to tissues add to compromised outer muscle capability.

Tending to smoking discontinuance is a critical part of muscular consideration, especially for people confronting medical procedures or overseeing persistent muscular circumstances. Perceiving the effect of smoking on outer muscle wellbeing underlines the requirement for social mediations focused on tobacco end to improve muscular results.

Hydration and Joint Wellbeing:

Legitimate hydration is a major component of muscular wellbeing, yet its importance is some of the time disregarded. Water is fundamental for the oil of joints, the vehicle of supplements to outer muscle tissues, and the end of byproducts. Lacking hydration can add to joint solidness, diminished adaptability, and an expanded gamble of wounds.

People participated in proactive tasks or those overseeing muscular circumstances are urged to keep up with appropriate hydration levels. Hydration upholds the versatility and usefulness of the outer muscle framework, adding to ideal joint wellbeing.

Stress The board and Outer muscle Effect:

The effect of weight on outer muscle wellbeing stretches out past its impact on mental prosperity. Constant pressure can add to muscle strain, irritation, and modified torment insight, all of which have suggestions for muscular health. Stress-related conditions, like pressure migraines and temporomandibular joint (TMJ) messes, feature the interconnected idea of stress and outer muscle wellbeing.

Integrating pressure the board methodologies into muscular consideration plans becomes basic for tending to the diverse effect of weight on the outer muscle framework. Strategies, for example, care, unwinding works out, and mental social intercessions can add to both the counteraction and the board of muscular circumstances.

Rest Quality and Muscular Recuperation:

The social variable of rest quality assumes a crucial part in the body's capacity to recuperate and fix outer muscle tissues. During rest, the body goes through fundamental cycles, including the arrival of development chemical and the maintenance of harmed tissues. Insufficient or upset rest examples can think twice about processes, possibly blocking muscular recuperation.

People recuperating from muscular medical procedures or overseeing ongoing circumstances benefit from focusing on great rest cleanliness. Sufficient and quality rest adds to in general prosperity, supporting the body's regular cycles for outer muscle fix and recuperation.

Psychosocial Variables and Muscular Consideration Adherence:

The psychosocial parts of a singular's life, including emotional well-being, social help, and ways of dealing with hardship or stress, altogether impact adherence to muscular consideration plans. Conduct factors like inspiration, versatility, and the capacity to adapt to stressors add to a singular's obligation to restoration works out, way of life changes, and different parts of muscular consideration.

Medical services suppliers perceive the significance of understanding psychosocial elements to tailor care designs that line up with the singular's interesting conditions. Incorporating social intercessions, for example, guiding or support gatherings, into muscular consideration improves in general persistent commitment and adds to additional good results.

Patient Training and Strengthening:

Schooling assumes a significant part in enabling people to pursue informed social decisions that decidedly influence their muscular wellbeing. Patient instruction drives that underscore the meaning of way of life factors, legitimate body mechanics, and taking care of oneself add to a feeling of organization and obligation.

Enabled people are bound to effectively participate in ways of behaving that help muscular wellbeing, from sticking to practice regimens to arriving at informed conclusions about sustenance and way of life. Patient training fills in as an impetus for conduct change, encouraging a proactive way to deal with outer muscle wellbeing.

3.4 Strategies for Addressing Both Dimensions

Methodologies for All encompassing Muscular Consideration: Exploring the Exchange of Physical and Profound Aspects

In the domain of muscular consideration, perceiving the complex exchange among physical and profound aspects is fundamental for encouraging extensive prosperity. Resolving outer muscle issues requires an all encompassing methodology that objectives the actual parts of conditions as well as recognizes and takes care of the profound prosperity of people. This investigation dives into methodologies for exploring the exchange of the two aspects, guaranteeing a patient-focused and coordinated way to deal with muscular consideration.

Exhaustive Appraisal and Individualized Care Plans:

The groundwork of all encompassing muscular consideration settles upon an exhaustive evaluation that thinks about both physical and close to home viewpoints. Medical services suppliers should dive past the outer layer of side effects to figure out the more extensive setting of a singular's life. This includes investigating psychosocial variables, stressors, and close to home prosperity to make a nuanced comprehension of the individual all in all.

Individualized care plans rise out of this thorough appraisal, fitting intercessions to meet the remarkable necessities of every patient. Perceiving that muscular circumstances influence the body as well as the whole individual takes into consideration the advancement of designated procedures that address both the actual signs of the condition and the profound reactions it evokes.

Incorporated Psychological well-being Backing:

The mix of psychological well-being support inside muscular consideration is essential for tending to the close to home components of outer muscle issues. Muscular circumstances can bring out a scope of feelings, from dissatisfaction and nervousness to wretchedness and loss of certainty. Giving admittance to psychological wellness experts, like clinicians or guides, guarantees that people get the everyday reassurance important to explore these difficulties.

Psychosocial evaluations become vital parts of muscular consideration, permitting medical services suppliers to distinguish and address profound variables that might affect recuperation. Consolidating psychological wellness support not just guides in adapting to the profound parts of muscular circumstances yet additionally adds to worked on in general prosperity.

Patient Instruction on the Psyche Body Association:

Enabling patients with information about the brain body association is an extraordinary system for all encompassing muscular consideration. Teaching people about the exchange between close to home prosperity and actual wellbeing cultivates mindfulness and energizes dynamic cooperation in their own consideration.

Understanding how stress, feelings, and way of life decisions can impact outer muscle wellbeing prepares people to go with informed choices and take on ways of behaving that help by and large prosperity.

Patient training ought to reach out past the specialized parts of muscular circumstances to incorporate systems for stress the executives, sound way of life decisions, and the significance of close to home flexibility. By cultivating a more profound comprehension of the psyche body association, medical care suppliers add to the strengthening of patients in overseeing the two components of their wellbeing.

Fuse of Psyche Body Practices:

Mind-body rehearses assume a vital part in overcoming any barrier among physical and close to home prosperity inside the domain of muscular consideration. Methods like care, contemplation, and yoga offer comprehensive advantages by tending to both the actual side effects of outer muscle conditions and the close to home reactions they trigger.

Care, specifically, has earned respect for its adequacy in overseeing torment, diminishing pressure, and improving generally speaking prosperity. Incorporating these practices into recovery projects and care plans gives people devices to develop strength, deal with profound trouble, and advance a feeling of harmony among brain and body.

Coordinated effort Among Muscular and Emotional well-being Experts:

A cooperative methodology between muscular subject matter experts and psychological well-being experts is major for tending to the double components of outer muscle wellbeing. This cooperative model guarantees that people get thorough consideration that tends to both the physical and profound parts of their circumstances.

Muscular and psychological wellness experts can take part in joint appraisals, sharing experiences and working together on care designs that think about the interconnected idea of brain and body. Ordinary correspondence between these experts considers the recognizable proof of arising profound worries, changes in accordance with care plans, and a consistent reconciliation of the two aspects inside the treatment cycle.

Advancement of Active work for Close to home Prosperity:

Active work, past its advantages for outer muscle wellbeing, assumes a pivotal part in supporting close to home prosperity. Standard activity is related with the arrival of endorphins, synapses that add to a positive state of mind and diminished impression of torment. Furthermore, active work gives a valuable outlet to stress and tension, advancing generally speaking profound flexibility.

Fitting activity regimens to individual abilities and inclinations is critical to guaranteeing adherence and positive profound results. Whether through directed restoration practices or taking part in exercises like swimming, strolling, or yoga, the advancement of actual work turns into a double system for upgrading both physical and profound elements of prosperity.

All encompassing Aggravation The executives Approaches:

Torment the executives in muscular consideration requires an all encompassing methodology that recognizes the complex idea of agony. Past drug intercessions, techniques like mental conduct treatment, needle therapy, and back rub treatment can add to both the actual alleviation of agony and the close to home insight of overseeing ongoing uneasiness.

Mental social treatment, specifically, addresses the mental and close to home parts of agony insight, helping people reexamine pessimistic considerations and foster methods for dealing with stress. Coordinating these comprehensive agony the board approaches into muscular consideration plans perceives the interconnectedness of physical and profound encounters related with outer muscle torment.

Support Gatherings and Friend Connection:

The force of companion backing and association couldn't possibly be more significant in that frame of mind of muscular consideration. Laying out help gatherings or working with peer collaborations among people confronting comparative outer muscle difficulties gives a stage to shared encounters, compassion, and basic reassurance. Peer cooperation encourages a feeling of local area, lessening sensations of seclusion and advancing close to home prosperity.

Support gatherings can be especially useful for people overseeing persistent circumstances or those going through broad recovery. These gatherings make spaces for people to communicate feelings, share ways of dealing with stress, and gain bits of knowledge from others exploring comparable excursions. The feeling of brotherhood inside help bunches adds to an all encompassing way to deal with care.

Compassionate Correspondence and Shared Direction:

Viable correspondence between medical services suppliers and patients is a key part in the all encompassing way to deal with muscular consideration. Laying out compassionate and open lines of correspondence permits people to communicate their profound worries, fears, and assumptions. Medical services suppliers, thusly, can give direction, address close to home parts of care, and include patients in shared navigation.

Shared direction guarantees that people effectively take part in deciding their consideration plans, settling on informed decisions that line up with their qualities and inclinations. This cooperative methodology upgrades the general patient experience and adds to a feeling of organization in overseeing both the physical and profound elements of muscular wellbeing.

Consideration of Family and Social Emotionally supportive networks:

The job of family and social emotionally supportive networks is vital in comprehensive muscular consideration. Perceiving the effect of outer muscle conditions on the more extensive environment of a singular's life considers the consideration of relatives, companions, and parental figures in the consideration cycle. Drawing in these emotionally supportive networks encourages close to home prosperity and gives reasonable help with exploring the difficulties related with muscular issues.

Relatives can assume a significant part in offering profound help, helping with day to day exercises, and building up sure conduct decisions. Consideration of emotionally supportive networks in conversations about care plans and recovery techniques guarantees a cooperative and all encompassing methodology that reaches out past the bounds of clinical settings.

Follow-Up Care and Long haul Backing:

All encompassing muscular consideration reaches out past the prompt treatment stage, stressing the significance of long haul support and follow-up care. Ordinary registrations with medical services suppliers, both muscular and psychological wellbeing experts, take into consideration continuous appraisal of physical and close to home prosperity. Acclimations to mind plans can be made in light of advancing necessities and reactions to mediations.

Long haul backing might include intermittent psychosocial evaluations, proceeded with admittance to emotional wellness assets, and support of way of life procedures that advance in general prosperity. Perceiving muscular consideration as a continuum guarantees that people get progressing backing to explore the unique interchange of physical and close to home aspects all through their outer muscle wellbeing venture.

Chapter 4

Scoliosis Struggles

Scoliosis Battles: Exploring the Difficulties of Spinal Shape

Scoliosis, an ailment portrayed by an unusual ebb and flow of the spine, presents a horde of difficulties for people wrestling with its belongings. From the actual indications of spinal deformation to the close to home and social ramifications, scoliosis represents a complicated scene that requires extensive comprehension and backing. This investigation dives into the battles related with scoliosis, revealing insight into the complex idea of the condition and the excursion of those impacted.

Actual Difficulties:

The most clear and quick battles for people with scoliosis are the actual difficulties that go with the strange shape of the spine. The seriousness and area of the ebb and flow can change, influencing stance, equilibrium, and by and large outer muscle capability. Lopsided arrangement of the shoulders, hips, and ribcage is normal, prompting a noticeably misshaped outline.

Scoliosis might bring about uneasiness, torment, and restrictions in versatility. Exercises that require a fair spine, like standing or strolling for expanded periods, may become burdensome. As the bend advances, the gamble of confusions, like respiratory issues, increments, further heightening the actual weight.

People with scoliosis frequently fight with the requirement for versatile systems to adapt to the actual difficulties. Altered supports, active recuperation, and now and again, careful mediations become piece of the excursion toward dealing with the actual indications of scoliosis. The most common way of adjusting to these intercessions, while expecting to relieve the effect on day to day existence, is a critical part of the battles related with the condition.

Close to home Effect:

The close to home cost of scoliosis is significant, influencing people across different age gatherings. Youths, specifically, may wrestle with self-perception worries as the ebb and flow modifies their actual appearance during a basic period of character development. The perceivability of the distortion, particularly in the juvenile years, can add to hesitance, brought down confidence, and sensations of seclusion.

Social cooperations might be affected by the profound effect of scoliosis, as people explore the provokes of being seen contrastingly because of their spinal arch. Tormenting and prodding, tragically, are normal encounters for those with scoliosis, further intensifying the profound battles related with the condition.

Past puberty, grown-ups with scoliosis might face an alternate arrangement of inner difficulties. Adapting to persistent agony, likely impediments in exercises, and the continuous administration of the condition can add to sensations of dissatisfaction, uneasiness, and even sadness. The mental cost of scoliosis highlights the significance of tending to the actual perspectives as well as the close to home prosperity of people impacted.

Challenges in Determination and Treatment:

The excursion of scoliosis is frequently set apart by difficulties in finding and treatment. The condition might slip through the cracks in its beginning phases, particularly when the arch is unobtrusive or grows progressively. Routine screenings in schools assist with recognizing scoliosis at times, however others might get a finding just when the disfigurement turns out to be more articulated or suggestive.

The indicative interaction itself can be genuinely charged, as people and their families explore the vulnerabilities related with scoliosis. Affirming the analysis might include imaging concentrates like X-beams, and the expectation of results can add to uneasiness.

When analyzed, the treatment way fluctuates in light of elements like the seriousness of the curve, the age of the individual, and the potential for movement. For teenagers, propping is a typical mediation pointed toward forestalling further bend. Nonetheless, the possibility of wearing a support for expanded periods presents difficulties as far as solace, self-perception concerns, and adherence to the treatment plan.

In situations where the curve is extreme or keeps on advancing notwithstanding moderate measures, careful mediation might be suggested. Spinal combination, a technique that includes intertwining vertebrae to balance out the spine, is a typical careful methodology. The choice to go through a medical procedure brings its own arrangement of difficulties, incorporating the dangers related with the methodology, recuperation contemplations, and the possible effect on versatility.

Monetary and Access Difficulties:

The excursion with scoliosis isn't absent any trace of monetary and access difficulties. The expenses related with finding, treatment, and continuous administration can overwhelm people and their families. Protection inclusion might fluctuate, and not all mediations might be completely covered, prompting monetary weights that add to the general difficulties of managing scoliosis.

Admittance to specific consideration, especially for those in underserved networks or locales with restricted medical services assets, can present huge difficulties. Ideal analysis, admittance to muscular subject matter experts, and accessibility of suitable intercessions might be compromised, affecting the general direction of scoliosis the executives.

For people without satisfactory monetary assets or extensive medical care, the battles related with scoliosis are compounded. The expected differences in admittance to quality consideration highlight the requirement for mindfulness, backing, and endeavors to guarantee that people confronting scoliosis get impartial and opportune help.

Influence on Day to day Exercises and Personal satisfaction:

Scoliosis can saturate different parts of day to day existence, impacting exercises that many underestimate. Straightforward undertakings like sitting serenely, representing broadened periods, or taking part in proactive tasks might become trying for those with scoliosis. The limits forced by the condition can stretch out to support in sports, sporting exercises, and, surprisingly, routine errands, adding to a feeling of dissatisfaction and limitation.

The effect on personal satisfaction isn't exclusively physical; it incorporates close to home prosperity, social associations, and the capacity to seek after one's inclinations and interests. People with scoliosis might end up exploring a fragile harmony between dealing with the actual difficulties and safeguarding a feeling of predictability in their regular routines.

Survival strategies and Versatility:

In the midst of the battles related with scoliosis, people frequently foster survival strategies and versatility that add to their capacity to explore the difficulties. Emotionally supportive networks, including family, companions, and friend gatherings, assume an essential part in offering profound help and understanding. Imparting encounters to others confronting comparative battles cultivates a feeling of local area and decreases the feeling of detachment.

Advising and emotional wellness support are significant parts of the adapting system. Tending to the profound effect of scoliosis and giving instruments to oversee pressure, uneasiness, and confidence concerns add to generally versatility. Empowering open correspondence about the difficulties confronted and advancing a positive outlook are fundamental parts of encouraging strength in people with scoliosis.

Support and Mindfulness Endeavors:

Promotion and mindfulness drives are fundamental parts of tending to the battles related with scoliosis on a more extensive scale. Expanding public mindfulness about the condition dissipates fantasies, lessen shame, and cultivate understanding. Promotion endeavors intend to guarantee that people with scoliosis approach opportune conclusion, proper mediations, and exhaustive help.

Support gatherings and associations devoted to scoliosis backing assume a urgent part in giving assets, data, and a stage for people to share their accounts. By intensifying the voices of those impacted by scoliosis, promotion endeavors add to a more comprehensive and compassionate comprehension of the difficulties related with the condition.

4.1 Understanding Scoliosis in Adolescents

Figuring out Scoliosis in Young people: An Extensive Investigation of Physical, Close to home, and Treatment Aspects

Scoliosis, an ailment described by a strange ebb and flow of the spine, takes on a particular importance when it appears in young people. This basic time of development and improvement adds layers of intricacy to the experience of scoliosis, enveloping actual difficulties, profound effect, and remarkable contemplations in conclusion and treatment. This investigation plans to give a far reaching comprehension of scoliosis in teenagers, revealing insight into the multi-layered aspects that shape the excursion of those impacted.

Actual Aspects:

The actual elements of scoliosis in teenagers are key to the comprehension of the condition. Scoliosis can appear in shifting levels of seriousness, and the unusual curve of the spine frequently becomes evident during times of quick development, like pubescence. The arch might grow steadily, making early discovery testing without routine screenings or careful perception.

The spine, in a sound state, ought to display a straight arrangement when seen from the front and have delicate bends when seen from the side. In scoliosis, notwithstanding, the spine strays from this standard, shaping a sideways ebb and flow. This deviation can influence the arrangement of the shoulders, hips, and ribcage, prompting noticeable unevenness.

Young people with scoliosis might encounter actual uneasiness, especially as the shape advances. The strange spinal arrangement can strain muscles, tendons, and joints, adding to impressions of agony or snugness. Exercises that include delayed times of sitting or standing might fuel these side effects, affecting day to day existence and by and large portability.

Routine exercises like conveying a rucksack, partaking in sports, or sitting for expanded periods in a homeroom can present difficulties for teenagers with scoliosis. The actual effect reaches out past simple distress; in serious cases, scoliosis can influence respiratory capability, possibly affecting lung limit and generally speaking wellbeing.

The seriousness of scoliosis is in many cases characterized by the level of arch, estimated in degrees utilizing the Cobb point. Gentle cases might require observing and painless intercessions, while additional extreme cases might require careful mediation to forestall further movement and address related difficulties.

Close to home Aspects:

The close to home elements of scoliosis in teenagers are entwined with the noticeable effect on actual appearance during a basic period of personality development. The perceivability of the spinal deformation can add to hesitance, self-perception concerns, and changes in confidence. Youths are especially powerless against the social elements that frequently go with apparent contrasts in actual appearance.

Exploring the profound scene of scoliosis includes tending to the immediate effect on self-insight as well as the potential for peer connections and cultural assumptions to impact the close to home prosperity of teenagers. Self-perception concerns might prompt a hesitance to take part in exercises that cause to notice the spinal ebb and flow, possibly influencing social commitment and cooperation in extracurricular exercises.

Teenagers with scoliosis might wrestle with sensations of detachment or a feeling of being not quite the same as their companions. The profound battles might stretch out past the person to incorporate worries and stresses communicated by guardians or parental figures. The psychosocial effect of scoliosis highlights the significance of all encompassing consideration that tends to both the physical and close to home components of the condition.

Harassing and Social Elements:

The apparent idea of scoliosis can make youths defenseless to harassing or prodding, further escalating the inner difficulties related with the condition. Peers, frequently ignorant about the clinical parts of scoliosis, may offer destructive remarks or participate in vilifying ways of behaving. This social dynamic can add to sensations of disgrace, shame, and a longing to disguise the spinal bend.

Instructive conditions, where youths spend a huge piece of their time, can assume a significant part in molding the social encounters of those with scoliosis. Making mindfulness and encouraging a steady and comprehensive air can moderate the effect of social difficulties on youths impacted by scoliosis.

Tormenting Counteraction and Instruction:

Endeavors to forestall harassing and advance instruction about scoliosis are fundamental parts of an extensive way to deal with supporting youths with the condition. Schools and instructive establishments can carry out programs that bring issues to light about scoliosis, encouraging compassion and understanding among understudies and teachers.

Giving instructive materials that make sense of the clinical parts of scoliosis, stressing that it's anything but a consequence of way of life decisions or ways of behaving, can add to a more educated and merciful school local area. Establishing a climate where contrasts are commended as opposed to criticized decreases the potential for harassing and prodding, permitting teenagers with scoliosis to explore their school a long time with more noteworthy certainty.

Analysis Difficulties and Ideal Intercession:

Diagnosing scoliosis in teenagers presents remarkable difficulties, as the condition may not be quickly clear, particularly in its beginning phases. Routine screenings, frequently directed in schools, assume a pivotal part in the early discovery of scoliosis. Nonetheless, not all teenagers might go through such screenings, and unpretentious bends might slip by everyone's notice without a far reaching assessment.

Guardians, parental figures, and medical services suppliers ought to stay careful for indications of scoliosis, including lopsided shoulders, hips, or the presence of a noticeable spinal bend. Standard check-ups, especially during development sprays, give valuable open doors to medical services experts to survey spinal wellbeing and intercede quickly assuming scoliosis is thought.

The indicative interaction might include imaging concentrates, for example, X-beams to precisely quantify the level of curve. When analyzed, the movement of scoliosis in youths requires cautious checking, particularly during times of quick development. Ordinary subsequent meetings with muscular experts assist with following changes in the curve and guide mediations in view of the singular's one of a kind conditions.

Harmless Mediations:

For gentle to direct instances of scoliosis in youths, harmless mediations might be prescribed to forestall further movement and oversee related side effects.

One normal mediation is the utilization of supports, intended to help the spine and relieve the improvement of a more serious curve. Propping is especially compelling when started during times of development, planning to direct the spine into a more typical arrangement.

Supporting, nonetheless, represents its own arrangement of difficulties for teenagers. Wearing a support for a few hours every day can influence day to day exercises, remembering cooperation for sports, social collaborations, and the choice of dress. The profound ramifications of wearing a support might need extra help, underlining the significance of tending to the all encompassing necessities of teenagers going through such mediations.

Mental Help and Survival techniques:

Mental help is a significant part of scoliosis the board in young people. Teenagers might profit from guiding or mental administrations that address self-perception concerns, confidence issues, and profound prosperity. Giving a place of refuge to young people to communicate their sentiments, fears, and goals can add to a positive mentality and strength in adapting to the difficulties of scoliosis.

Survival methods customized to the extraordinary requirements of young people with scoliosis assume a urgent part in cultivating profound prosperity. Empowering open correspondence with peers, relatives, and medical care suppliers adds to a strong organization that comprehends and recognizes the profound elements of scoliosis.

Influence on Day to day Exercises and Social Commitment:

The effect of scoliosis on day to day exercises and social commitment is a critical part of the juvenile involvement in the condition. Teenagers might end up changing in accordance with oblige the actual difficulties presented by scoliosis, whether it be taking on unambiguous stances, picking suitable seating, or altering exercises to limit distress.

Cooperation in sports and proactive tasks might require cautious thought to guarantee that teenagers with scoliosis can connect securely and serenely. While specific high-effect or physical games might introduce difficulties, numerous people with scoliosis find satisfaction and delight in exercises that line up with their capacities and interests.

Tending to the effect of scoliosis on everyday exercises and social commitment includes cultivating a feeling of independence and empowering youths to investigate exercises that give pleasure and satisfaction. Versatile methodologies and backing from medical services suppliers can add to a climate where young people feel engaged to explore their regular routines with certainty.

Careful Intercessions:

In situations where scoliosis advances to a serious degree and harmless mediations demonstrate lacking, careful mediations might be thought of. Spinal combination, a typical surgery for scoliosis, includes intertwining vertebrae to balance out the spine and forestall further curve.

Careful mediations are critical achievements in the excursion of youths with scoliosis, requiring cautious thought of the likely advantages, dangers, and effect on personal satisfaction. The choice to go through a medical procedure frequently includes coordinated effort between medical care suppliers, youths, and their families, considering the special conditions of every person.

Post-careful recuperation is a basic stage that needs progressing help and restoration. Young people might confront physical and personal difficulties during this period, remembering acclimations to changes for spinal arrangement, the utilization of steady gadgets, and recovery activities to reestablish versatility.

Instructive Backing and Backing:

Given the expected effect of scoliosis on instructive encounters, backing for instructive help is vital for youths with the condition. Instructive foundations can assume a proactive part in guaranteeing that facilities are set up to address the special requirements of understudies with scoliosis.

Adaptable guest plans, admittance to steady furnishings, and contemplations for proactive tasks can add to a positive instructive encounter for young people with scoliosis. Cooperation between teachers, medical care suppliers, and guardians works with a comprehensive way to deal with supporting scholarly accomplishment while dealing with the difficulties related with the condition.

Parental and Guardian Job:

The job of guardians and parental figures is foremost in the excursion of teenagers with scoliosis. Past offering physical and close to home help, guardians assume an essential part in upholding for their youngster's necessities inside instructive settings, medical care conditions, and the more extensive local area.

Open correspondence between guardians, teenagers, and medical care suppliers encourages a cooperative way to deal with scoliosis the board. Understanding the remarkable difficulties looked by young people and giving a steady climate at home adds to strength and positive results.

4.2 Causes and Risk Factors

Causes and Hazard Variables of Scoliosis: Unwinding the Complicated Snare of Spinal Curve Starting points

Scoliosis, portrayed by an unusual sidelong shape of the spine, is a multi-layered condition with beginnings established in a mix of hereditary, formative, and natural variables. Understanding the causes and chance variables of scoliosis is critical for early identification, mediation, and the improvement of designated administration techniques. This investigation dives into the perplexing trap of impacts that add to the improvement of scoliosis.

Hereditary Variables:

Hereditary inclination assumes a huge part in the improvement of scoliosis. Research demonstrates that people with a family background of scoliosis have a higher probability of fostering the actual condition. While the exact hereditary instruments stay a subject of continuous review, obviously there is a genetic part that adds to the gamble of scoliosis.

Explicit qualities related with scoliosis vulnerability have been recognized, albeit the legacy example can fluctuate. Hereditary elements might impact the manner in which the spine structures during fetal turn of events, affecting its development and arrangement. Varieties in quality articulation connected with bone and ligament improvement might add to the underlying changes saw in scoliosis.

Formative Elements:

The formative time frame, especially during outset and youth, is a basic window for the development and arrangement of the spine. Aggravations in this cycle can prompt the improvement of scoliosis. Intrinsic scoliosis, for instance, is connected to anomalies in the arrangement of the vertebrae during the beginning phases of fetal turn of events.

Neuromuscular scoliosis is another sort that can emerge from conditions influencing the nerves and muscles, like cerebral paralysis or solid dystrophy. Deviated muscle advancement or shortcoming in specific muscle gatherings can add to an awkwardness that influences the arrangement of the spine. In these cases, tending to the hidden neuromuscular condition is fundamental in overseeing scoliosis.

Idiopathic Scoliosis:

Idiopathic scoliosis, which represents most of scoliosis cases, is a term utilized when the specific reason is obscure. This type of scoliosis commonly arises during puberty and may advance during times of quick development. Regardless of the shortfall of a reasonable reason, there are perceived gamble factors related with idiopathic scoliosis.

Age and sex are huge variables, with juvenile young ladies having a higher gamble of creating scoliosis than young men. The beginning of idiopathic scoliosis frequently happens around the hour of pubescence, recommending a possible connection between hormonal changes and the condition. Hormonal elements, like those connected with development and pubescence, are areas of dynamic examination in figuring out the starting points of idiopathic scoliosis.

Neuromuscular Circumstances:

Scoliosis can be auxiliary to different neuromuscular circumstances that influence muscle tone and coordination. Conditions like cerebral paralysis, strong dystrophy, or spinal solid decay can bring about muscle irregular characteristics that influence the arrangement of the spine. People with neuromuscular scoliosis frequently require thorough administration that tends to the hidden condition close by spinal shape.

Neuromuscular scoliosis will in general present at a previous age than idiopathic scoliosis, and its movement might be more fast. Observing and overseeing neuromuscular circumstances from a beginning phase are significant for tending to the related gamble of scoliosis and alleviating its effect on in general wellbeing and capability.

Connective Tissue Problems:

Certain connective tissue problems can incline people toward scoliosis. Conditions like Marfan disorder and Ehlers-Danlos disorder, described by modifications in the design of connective tissues, may influence the tendons and plates supporting the spine. The laxity of these tissues can add to spinal insecurity and curve.

Connective tissue problems frequently include fundamental appearances, and resolving the basic hereditary or underlying issues is essential in overseeing scoliosis in these cases. Cooperative consideration including experts in hereditary qualities, muscular health, and other pertinent disciplines is fundamental for an exhaustive way to deal with people with scoliosis related with connective tissue problems.

Postural and Utilitarian Causes:

Not all types of spinal arch are obsessive; some might be connected with postural propensities or utilitarian elements. Non-primary scoliosis, otherwise called utilitarian scoliosis, happens when the spine seems bended, yet there is no basic underlying anomaly. This sort of scoliosis might result from variables like muscle lopsided characteristics, leg length disparities, or constant awry stacking of the spine.

Tending to postural and practical causes includes mediations, for example, active recuperation, activities to address muscle lopsided characteristics, and orthotic support in the event that leg length disparities are available. Recognizing underlying and non-primary scoliosis is urgent in deciding the proper course of the executives.

Natural Variables:

While hereditary and formative elements assume noticeable parts in scoliosis, ecological variables may likewise add to the gamble of movement. Quick development sprays during youthfulness can fuel the bend in people inclined toward scoliosis. The impact of ecological elements is especially clear in idiopathic scoliosis, where the condition frequently becomes obvious during times of quick skeletal development.

Word related and way of life variables may likewise assume a part, particularly in instances of grown-up beginning degenerative scoliosis. Delayed times of unfortunate stance, word related requests that include dreary awry developments, or elements that add to spinal degeneration can impact the improvement of scoliosis sometime down the road.

Lopsidedness in Appendage Length:

Leg length errors, where one leg is more limited than the other, can add to the turn of events or movement of scoliosis. The body might adjust to the disparity in appendage length by changing pelvic arrangement and spinal ebb and flow. This versatile reaction can prompt a scoliotic bend as the spine endeavors to keep up with balance within the sight of leg length deviation.

Tending to leg length disparities might include orthotic intercessions, for example, shoe lifts, to reestablish harmony and decrease the effect on spinal arrangement. Legitimate evaluation and the board of appendage length imbalances are fundamental parts of a far reaching way to deal with scoliosis, particularly in situations where practical variables add to the bend.

Orientation Differences:

Scoliosis displays eminent orientation variations, with juvenile young ladies at a higher gamble of fostering the condition than young men. The explanations for this orientation disparity are not completely perceived, yet hormonal variables have been embroiled. The beginning of scoliosis frequently matches with the juvenile development spray, a period described by huge hormonal changes.

Estrogen, specifically, has been recommended as a potential hormonal variable impacting the improvement of scoliosis. Research demonstrates that hormonal receptors are available in the tissues encompassing the spine, and estrogen might affect bone development and redesigning. The perplexing transaction between chemicals, development factors, and hereditary inclination highlights the multifactorial idea of scoliosis in young adult young ladies.

4.3 Emotional Toll of Scoliosis

The Profound Cost of Scoliosis: Exploring the Mind boggling Scene of Mental Effect

Scoliosis, with its actual sign of a horizontal curve of the spine, expands its effect past the domain of the simply physiological.

The profound cost of scoliosis is a complex and frequently disregarded aspect that essentially impacts the existences of people wrestling with this condition. This investigation expects to dive into the multi-layered personal difficulties looked by those with scoliosis, revealing insight into the mental complexities that go with the actual excursion.

Self-perception Concerns and Confidence:

One of the most articulated inner difficulties related with scoliosis rotates around self-perception concerns and confidence. The noticeable deformation brought about by the unusual curve of the spine can prompt identity cognizance and, now and again, significant effects on confidence. Young people, specifically, may end up exploring this part of scoliosis during a basic period of character development.

The ebb and flow changes the normal evenness of the body, influencing the arrangement of the shoulders, hips, and ribcage. This noticeable unevenness can be moving for people to acknowledge, prompting an increased familiarity with their actual contrasts. Self-perception concerns might saturate different parts of life, impacting clothing decisions, act, and the eagerness to participate in exercises that cause to notice the spinal deformation.

Tending to self-perception concerns requires a comprehensive methodology that envelops basic encouragement, guiding, and techniques to cultivate a positive mental self view. Establishing a strong climate that urges people to embrace their uniqueness while giving devices to explore cultural view of magnificence and business as usual is critical in relieving the effect on confidence.

Social Elements and Friend Cooperations:

The social elements encompassing scoliosis can be mind boggling, especially in youthfulness where peer collaborations assume a focal part in molding character and having a place. The noticeable idea of scoliosis can make people defenseless to the look and decisions of others, possibly affecting social communications. Harassing and prodding, sadly, are normal encounters for those with scoliosis, adding an extra layer of profound pressure.

Young people might wrestle with the apprehension about being vilified or rejected in view of their actual appearance. The longing to fit in and be acknowledged by friends can be elevated, and people with scoliosis might take extraordinary measures to hide their spinal ebb and flow or keep away from circumstances where their condition might turn into a subject of conversation.

Instructive conditions, where young people spend a critical piece of their time, can either be steady or trying for people with scoliosis. Mindfulness programs, anti-bullying drives, and encouraging a comprehensive culture add to a positive social environment. Teaching peers about scoliosis and advancing compassion can assist with destroying confusions and lessen the potential for social detachment.

Influence on Psychological wellness:

The close to home cost of scoliosis can reach out to psychological wellness, with people confronting an expanded gamble of tension and gloom. The consistent consciousness of a noticeable disfigurement, combined with the cultural tensions to adjust to regular guidelines of excellence, can add to elevated feelings of anxiety and close to home pain.

Youths, specifically, may wrestle with the intricacies of self-personality and self-esteem, with scoliosis possibly worsening the difficulties related with puberty. The profound effect can appear as sensations of trouble, dissatisfaction, or a feeling of weakness. In serious cases, untreated close to home misery can advance into more critical emotional wellness challenges, highlighting the significance of early mediation and psychological well-being support.

Perceiving the interconnectedness of physical and mental prosperity in people with scoliosis is critical. An exhaustive way to deal with care ought to include psychological wellness evaluations, guiding administrations, and techniques to upgrade flexibility and survival strategies. Making a place of refuge for people to communicate their feelings, fears, and goals encourages a steady climate helpful for mental prosperity.

Parental Worries and Guardian Jobs:

The profound cost of scoliosis stretches out not exclusively to the people with the condition yet in addition to their folks and parental figures. Seeing a kid explore the inner difficulties of scoliosis can summon sensations of concern, sympathy, and a profound longing to lighten the close to home weight. Guardians might wrestle with their own profound reactions, including stresses over their youngster's prosperity, the expected effect on their public activity, and the drawn out mental ramifications.

The parental figure job goes past offering actual help; it includes being sensitive to the feelings of people with scoliosis. Open correspondence, undivided attention, and cultivating a strong family climate add to the profound prosperity of people wrestling with scoliosis. Guardians and parental figures assume significant parts in supporting for their kid's feelings inside instructive settings, medical services conditions, and the more extensive local area.

Psychosocial Backing and Methods for dealing with especially difficult times:

Psychosocial support is a basic part in tending to the close to home cost of scoliosis. Support gatherings, either face to face or on the web, give a stage to people to share their encounters, trade survival methods, and construct a feeling of local area. Interfacing with other people who have confronted comparative difficulties encourages a feeling of understanding and diminishes the feeling of detachment.

Advising and emotional well-being administrations custom-made to the special necessities of people with scoliosis are important assets.

These administrations address self-perception concerns, confidence issues, and give apparatuses to oversee pressure, tension, and misery. Psychosocial backing ought to be incorporated into the general consideration plan, perceiving the significance of tending to close to home prosperity close by actual wellbeing.

Empowering the improvement of survival techniques is fundamental in engaging people to explore the close to home intricacies of scoliosis. Methods, for example, care, unwinding activities, and positive perception can add to close to home flexibility. Taking part in exercises that give pleasure and satisfaction, whether they are creative, sporting, or social, upgrades the general prosperity of people with scoliosis.

Instructive Promotion and Mindfulness Drives:

Instructive promotion and mindfulness drives are instrumental in tending to the profound cost of scoliosis inside instructive conditions. Educators, school staff, and friends benefit from understanding the psychosocial challenges related with scoliosis.

Executing programs that advance compassion, inclusivity, and mindfulness about the condition makes a more steady climate for people with scoliosis.

Integrating instructive materials about scoliosis into the educational program disperses fantasies, decrease disgrace, and cultivate understanding. Mindfulness drives can incorporate introductions, studios, or data meetings that instruct understudies and teachers about the physical and close to home components of scoliosis. By normalizing contrasts and advancing a culture of acknowledgment, instructive conditions become spaces where people with scoliosis feel esteemed and upheld.

The Job of Medical services Suppliers:

Medical services suppliers, especially muscular subject matter experts and unified wellbeing experts, assume a crucial part in tending to the profound cost of scoliosis. Viable correspondence, sympathy, and a patient-focused approach are fundamental in making a helpful collusion that reaches out past the actual parts of care.

Medical services suppliers ought to regularly ask about the profound prosperity of people with scoliosis during clinical visits. Giving assets to psychological well-being support, directing administrations, and interfacing people with peer support bunches are necessary parts of all encompassing consideration. Recognizing the inner difficulties and approving the sensations of people with scoliosis add to a sympathetic and patient-driven medical care insight.

4.4 Treatment Options and Coping Strategies

Treatment Choices and Survival methods for Scoliosis: Exploring the Way to Physical and Profound Prosperity

Scoliosis, portrayed by a strange horizontal curve of the spine, requires a diverse way to deal with treatment that tends to both the physical and profound components of the condition. This investigation intends to clarify the different treatment choices accessible and survival techniques utilized by people with scoliosis, stressing the significance of an all encompassing way to deal with cultivate generally prosperity.

Painless Mediations:

For gentle to direct instances of scoliosis, painless mediations are in many cases the underlying line of treatment. Among these, propping is a usually utilized strategy to end the movement of spinal bend, especially during times of quick development in pre-adulthood. Supports, tweaked to the singular's arch, are intended to offer help and urge the spine to adjust all the more regularly.

While viable in forestalling further movement, propping can introduce difficulties, particularly for teenagers. Consistence with wearing the support for a few hours every day can affect day to day exercises, cooperation in sports, and, surprisingly, the decision of dress. The profound ramifications of wearing a support, including worries about self-perception, ought to be tended to close by the actual advantages.

Exercise based recuperation is another harmless mediation that assumes a critical part in scoliosis the board. Remedial activities center around further developing muscle strength, adaptability, and generally speaking spinal security. Actual advisors work with people to foster customized practice regimens custom-made to their particular curve and utilitarian capacities.

Instruction about stance and body mechanics is an indispensable part of active recuperation. People learn methods to enhance spinal arrangement in different exercises, lessening the burden on the spine and relieving distress. Enabling people with information about their condition improves their capacity to take part in their consideration effectively.

Mental Help and Survival techniques:

Mental help is an essential part of scoliosis the board, perceiving the inner difficulties that frequently go with the actual parts of the condition. Guiding and treatment furnish people with scoliosis a place of refuge to investigate their sentiments, address self-perception concerns, and foster survival techniques for exploring the intricacies of day to day existence.

Mental social treatment (CBT) is one methodology that can be especially advantageous. CBT helps people recognize and alter pessimistic idea designs and foster compelling survival techniques. It outfits people with the instruments to oversee pressure, uneasiness, and the profound effect of living with scoliosis.

Peer support bunches offer a significant wellspring of association and understanding. Sharing encounters, difficulties, and wins with other people who have confronted or are confronting comparable circumstances encourages a feeling of local area and decreases sensations of detachment. These gatherings offer close to home help as well as viable experiences into survival methods that have worked for other people.

Family treatment may likewise be advantageous, particularly when scoliosis influences teenagers. Remembering relatives for the remedial cycle improves correspondence, addresses familial worries, and reinforces the general emotionally supportive network. Guardians and parental figures assume essential parts in offering close to home help and ought to be effectively engaged with the survival methods of the person with scoliosis.

Mind-Body Procedures:

Mind-body procedures include a scope of practices that emphasis on the association between the psyche and the body. These strategies plan to advance unwinding, diminish pressure, and improve generally prosperity. With regards to scoliosis, mind-body approaches can supplement conventional medicines and add to an all encompassing methodology.

Yoga is one such brain body practice that underlines delicate extending, fortifying, and unwinding. Variations can be made to oblige individual necessities and constraints, making yoga open for people with scoliosis. Participating in normal yoga practice might assist with further developing adaptability, ease muscle strain, and advance a feeling of equilibrium.

Reflection and care strategies are significant devices for overseeing pressure and tension related with scoliosis. Care includes developing present-second mindfulness without judgment. Integrating care rehearses into day to day existence can upgrade close to home flexibility, diminish the effect of negative considerations, and add to a general feeling of prosperity.

Intrusive Mediations:

In situations where scoliosis advances to an extreme degree or harmless mediations demonstrate deficient, careful intercessions might be thought of. Spinal combination, a typical surgery for scoliosis, includes melding vertebrae to settle the spine and forestall further shape. Careful choices are ordinarily made in view of elements like the level of curve, the probability of movement, and the effect on the singular's general wellbeing.

Medical procedure is a huge move toward the therapy excursion of people with scoliosis, and the choice to go through a medical procedure requires cautious thought. Muscular specialists team up with people and their families to gauge the possible advantages of a medical procedure against the dangers and recuperation process. The mental effect of a medical procedure, including worries about self-perception and changes in accordance with postoperative changes, ought to be tended to in preoperative conversations.

Post-careful recuperation is a basic stage that includes recovery, non-intrusive treatment, and continuous help. People might encounter a scope of feelings during this period, from help at the remedy of the ebb and flow to changes in self-perception and actual capability. A complete way to deal with post-careful attention incorporates tending to both the physical and profound parts of recuperation.

Versatile Systems for Day to day Living:

Adjusting to the difficulties of day to day living with scoliosis includes consolidating methodologies that upgrade solace and usefulness. Ergonomic adjustments in the home and work environment can lessen burden on the spine. Utilizing strong seats, enhancing work area arrangements, and picking proper seating are pragmatic contemplations that add to day to day prosperity.

Versatile gadgets, like strong pads or pads, can improve solace during delayed times of sitting or resting. People with scoliosis might find explicit dozing positions more agreeable, and the selection of sleeping cushions and pads can be custom fitted to individual inclinations.

Participating in ordinary actual work that lines up with the singular's capacities is significant for generally wellbeing. Low-influence works out, like swimming or strolling, can assist with keeping up with cardiovascular wellness without applying exorbitant tension on the spine. Work-out schedules ought to be created in discussion with medical care suppliers to guarantee they are protected and custom fitted to the particular necessities of people with scoliosis.

Instructive Promotion and Backing:

Instructive support is fundamental for people with scoliosis, especially in scholarly settings. Instructive organizations ought to know about the special requirements of understudies with scoliosis and give essential facilities. Adaptable guest plans, admittance to steady furnishings, and contemplations for proactive tasks add to a positive instructive encounter.

Support from instructors and mindfulness among peers are fundamental parts of establishing a comprehensive instructive climate. Executing hostile to harassing drives, instructing understudies about scoliosis, and encouraging compassion can add to a culture where people with scoliosis feel acknowledged and upheld.

Individualized schooling plans (IEPs) or 504 plans can be created to address explicit scholar and actual necessities. These plans frame facilities, changes, and backing administrations that guarantee people with scoliosis have equivalent admittance to instructive open doors. Normal correspondence between guardians, instructors, and medical services suppliers is essential for the viable execution of these plans.

All encompassing Way of life Approaches:

Comprehensive way of life approaches include a scope of practices that add to by and large prosperity. Nourishment assumes a fundamental part in supporting bone wellbeing and generally speaking actual capability. People with scoliosis ought to guarantee a reasonable eating regimen that incorporates satisfactory calcium, vitamin D, and other fundamental supplements. Sustenance meetings with medical services experts can give customized direction.

Keeping a sound weight is significant for overseeing scoliosis, as overabundance weight can fuel the burden on the spine. Normal active work, adjusted to individual abilities, adds to generally speaking wellbeing and may assist with lightening muscle strain and uneasiness related with scoliosis.

All encompassing methodologies may likewise include correlative treatments, for example, chiropractic care, needle therapy, or back rub treatment. While the adequacy of these treatments differs, a few people track down help from side effects and improved prosperity through correlative methodologies. It is fundamental to talk with medical care suppliers prior to integrating reciprocal treatments into the general therapy plan.

Chapter 5

Sports Injuries and Emotional Resilience

Sports Wounds and Close to home Flexibility: Exploring the Convergence of Actual Mishaps and Mental Strength

Taking part in sports offers various physical and emotional wellness benefits, encouraging discipline, cooperation, and a pride. Notwithstanding, the quest for athletic undertakings additionally accompanies innate dangers, and sports wounds can present huge difficulties to a singular's prosperity. This investigation digs into the complicated connection between sports wounds and profound versatility, featuring the significance of mental strength despite actual misfortunes.

The Actual Cost of Sports Wounds:

Sports wounds can go from minor injuries and strains to additional serious circumstances, for example, cracks, tendon tears, and blackouts. The actual cost of these wounds frequently stretches out past the quick agony and distress, affecting a competitor's capacity to perform, contend, and, at times, seek after their enthusiasm briefly or even forever.

The way to recuperation might include recovery, clinical intercessions, and acclimations to preparing regimens.

One of the provokes competitors face is the disturbance to their daily practice and the vulnerability encompassing the course of events for return to play. This interference can prompt disappointment, uneasiness, and a feeling of misfortune, particularly for those profoundly put resources into their game. The actual cost, combined with the mental effect of being sidelined, highlights the requirement for an extensive way to deal with sports injury the executives that incorporates both physical and mental prosperity.

The Close to home Effect of Sports Wounds:

The close to home effect of sports wounds can be significant, influencing competitors at different degrees of rivalry. For proficient competitors, whose livelihoods are frequently attached to their actual presentation, a lot is on the line. The apprehension about losing sponsorships, contracts, or the capacity to contend at the first class level increases the profound weight. At the university and beginner levels, competitors might wrestle with the feeling of personality attached to their game, social elements inside their athletic networks, and the more extensive ramifications for their future in the game.

Normal close to home reactions to sports wounds incorporate melancholy, dissatisfaction, outrage, and uneasiness. Competitors might grieve the deficiency of their actual capacities, the expectation of contests, and the fellowship of their group. Dissatisfaction emerges from the apparent absence of command over the circumstance and the vulnerability of the recuperation interaction. Tension about the future, anxiety toward reinjury, and worries about falling behind in expertise advancement add to the personal difficulties competitors face.

The Job of Profound Strength:

Profound strength is a urgent calculate exploring the complicated landscape of sports wounds. Characterized as the capacity to adjust and return quickly from misfortune, strength enables competitors to adapt to difficulties, keep a positive mentality, and effectively participate in their recuperation. Strength includes returning as well as gaining and developing from the experience, arising more grounded and more clever.

Strong competitors show specific attributes that add to their capacity to successfully adapt to sports wounds:

Positive Mentality: Tough competitors keep an uplifting perspective, zeroing in on what they have some control over as opposed to harping on the limits forced by the injury. Embracing a development mentality, where difficulties are viewed as any open doors for learning and improvement, upgrades the capacity to explore difficulties.

Versatility: Strength includes flexibility and adaptability even with difficulty. Competitors who can change their objectives, preparing schedules, and assumptions during the recuperation interaction show an ability to explore the vulnerabilities related with sports wounds.

Compelling Survival techniques: Creating sound methods for dealing with stress is fundamental for profound flexibility. This might incorporate looking for help from colleagues, mentors, or emotional well-being experts, as well as participating in exercises that give pleasure and satisfaction beyond the game.

Objective Setting: Defining practical and feasible objectives all through the recuperation cycle adds to a feeling of direction and progress. Strong competitors separate their excursion into reasonable advances, celebrating little triumphs en route.

Social Help: The help of partners, mentors, companions, and family assumes a urgent part in building close to home versatility. A solid emotionally supportive network gives consolation, compassion, and a feeling of having a place, assisting competitors with exploring the inner difficulties of injury.

Close to home Guideline: Strong competitors foster profound guideline abilities, permitting them to recognize and communicate their feelings while keeping up with command over their reactions. This includes perceiving negative contemplations and reexamining them in a more certain light.

Building Close to home Flexibility in Competitors:
Building profound versatility is a powerful cycle that includes purposeful endeavors, emotionally supportive networks, and a guarantee to mental prosperity. Competitors, mentors, and sports associations can find proactive ways to encourage profound flexibility inside the wearing local area:

Psychological well-being Schooling: Integrating psychological well-being training into sports programs assists competitors with figuring out the mental parts of sports wounds and the significance of profound prosperity. Destigmatizing emotional wellness conversations establishes an open climate for competitors to look for help.

Admittance to Emotional wellness Experts: Sports associations ought to focus on giving admittance to psychological well-being experts who represent considerable authority in working with competitors. These experts can offer guiding, mental help, and survival methods custom fitted to the novel difficulties of sports wounds.

Group Holding and Correspondence: Developing areas of strength for an of group holding and open correspondence inside athletic groups establishes a steady climate. Competitors who feel associated with their colleagues are bound to share their battles and look for help when required.

Versatility Preparing Projects: Executing strength preparing programs as a feature of the general competitor improvement educational plan outfits competitors with abilities to explore difficulties. These projects might incorporate studios, classes, and down to earth practices zeroed in on building strength.

Groundwork for Difficulty: Mentors assume a urgent part in getting ready competitors for misfortune by imparting versatility as an esteemed quality. Stressing the significance of mental strength, versatility, and a positive outlook makes a culture where competitors are better prepared to confront misfortunes.

All encompassing Competitor Backing: Perceiving competitors as comprehensive people with physical, mental, and profound aspects illuminates an exhaustive way to deal with competitor support. Sports associations ought to focus on the general prosperity of competitors, including emotional well-being, in their arrangements and projects.

Get back to Game and Proceeded with Versatility:
The excursion of recuperation from a games injury comes full circle in the competitor's re-visitation of game. This stage includes a fragile harmony between actual preparation and mental readiness. Competitors might wrestle with the apprehension about reinjury, execution uneasiness, and the strain to live up to assumptions, both inward and outside.

The method involved with getting back to brandish needs progressing help, correspondence, and cooperation between competitors, mentors, and medical services experts. Competitors should be consoled that the inner difficulties they might insight during the re-visitation of game are ordinary and that looking for help is an indication of solidarity, not shortcoming.

Mentors assume a vital part in observing the profound prosperity of competitors during the re-visitation of game stage. Empowering open correspondence, changing assumptions, and recognizing the profound intricacies of the excursion add to a strong climate.

Proceeded with profound flexibility past the re-visitation of game is fundamental for long haul prosperity. Competitors might experience new difficulties, mishaps, or advances in their athletic professions. The abilities and systems created during the recuperation interaction act as important instruments for exploring future afflictions.

5.1 Common Sports-related Ortho Injuries in Teens

Normal Games related Muscular Wounds in Teenagers: Exploring the Actual Difficulties of Athletic Pursuits

Youthfulness is a powerful stage set apart by development sprays, expanded actual work, and cooperation in coordinated sports. While commitment in sports encourages actual wellness, collaboration, and discipline, it likewise opens youngsters to the gamble of muscular wounds. This investigation dives into the normal games related muscular wounds that influence youngsters, revealing insight into the sorts, causes, and possible preventive measures to explore the actual difficulties innate in athletic pursuits.

1. **Injuries and Strains:**

   Among the most predominant games related wounds in young people are injuries and strains. These wounds happen when tendons (injuries) or muscles and ligaments (strains) are extended or torn because of abrupt developments, abuse, or ill-advised strategies. Ordinarily impacted regions incorporate the lower legs, knees, and wrists. Adolescents engaged with sports that require fast course adjustments or regular hopping, like ball or soccer, are especially powerless.

   Preventive measures incorporate appropriate warm-up schedules, extending activities, and molding programs that improve adaptability and reinforce supporting muscles. Teaching youngsters about the significance of satisfactory rest between serious exercises is additionally essential in forestalling these wounds.

2. **Breaks:**

   Breaks, or broken bones, are one more predominant muscular injury among teenagers took part in sports. Influence from falls, crashes, or redundant weight on a specific bone can prompt cracks. Normal locales for breaks incorporate the wrist, lower arm, and collarbone. Teenagers taking part in physical games like football or exercises with a gamble of falls, like skating, face a raised gamble.

   Preventive measures include utilizing legitimate defensive stuff, like caps, cushions, and supports, contingent upon the game. Training staff ought to stress appropriate procedures and safe playing conditions to limit the gamble of cracks. Furthermore, integrating strength preparing activities can improve bone thickness and diminish defenselessness to breaks.

3. **Development Plate Wounds:**

The development plates, areas of creating ligament close to the closures of long bones, are helpless against wounds in developing youngsters. Monotonous pressure or awful effect can prompt development plate cracks or wounds, usually influencing the knees, elbows, and shoulders. Taking part in sports with a high gamble of effect, for example, vaulting or football, improves the probability of development plate wounds.

Preventive measures include age-suitable preparation programs that think about the continuous development and improvement of the skeletal framework. Mentors and coaches ought to know about the exceptional weaknesses related with development plates and designer practices in like manner. Legitimate rest stretches and checking for indications of abuse are fundamental in forestalling development plate wounds.

4. **Abuse Wounds:**

Abuse wounds result from monotonous weight on a specific piece of the body without adequate time for recuperation. In the young adult populace, abuse wounds frequently manifest as pressure cracks, tendinitis, or stress responses in bones. Sports that include monotonous movements, like running in olympic style events or tedious hopping in b-ball, add to the gamble of abuse wounds.

Forestalling abuse wounds requires a reasonable way to deal with preparing and rest. Mentors and coaches ought to empower appropriate warm-up, cooldown, and extending schedules. Carrying out broadly educating exercises that change the kinds of developments and weights on the body can decrease the gamble of abuse wounds. Youngsters ought to likewise be taught on the significance of paying attention to their bodies and detailing any indications of determined torment.

5. **Upper leg tendon Wounds:**

Foremost Cruciate Tendon (leg tendon) wounds, especially in the knee, are normal among young competitors, particularly in sports including abrupt stops, course adjustments, or hopping. Female competitors have a higher defenselessness to leg tendon wounds contrasted with their male partners. These wounds can go from gentle injuries to finish tears and frequently require careful intercession.

Preventive measures incorporate neuromuscular preparation programs that attention on further developing equilibrium, strength, and legitimate landing strategies. Training competitors to keep away from unsafe developments that put over the top weight on the leg tendon, like inappropriate arrivals or unexpected turns, is significant. Normal strength preparing to improve the security of the knee joint can likewise add to forestalling upper leg tendon wounds.

6. **Blackouts:**
While blackouts are not stringently muscular wounds, they are a huge worry in sports with a gamble of head wounds, like football, soccer, and hockey. Blackouts result from a hit to the head or an unexpected shock that makes the cerebrum move inside the skull. Young people are especially powerless because of the continuous improvement of their neurological frameworks.
Preventive measures incorporate severe adherence to somewhere safe and secure conventions, legitimate utilization of defensive headgear, and training on perceiving and detailing blackout side effects. Mentors, competitors, and guardians ought to focus on the security of youthful competitors, and any thought head injury ought to provoke quick assessment by medical care experts.

7. **Tendonitis:**
Tendonitis, aggravation of the ligaments, usually influences teenagers engaged with sports with dull movements, like tennis, baseball, or swimming. Abuse and ill-advised biomechanics add to the advancement of tendonitis. The shoulders, elbows, and knees are normal destinations for this condition.
Forestalling tendonitis includes executing appropriate preparation strategies and underscoring biomechanical productivity. Mentors ought to screen competitors for indications of abuse and mediate with changes to preparing schedules depending on the situation. Sufficient warm-up, cooldown, and extending practices likewise assume a critical part in forestalling tendonitis.

8. **Disengagements:**
Joint disengagements, where the bones in a joint are constrained out of their typical position, can happen in different games, especially those including contact or unexpected effects. Ordinarily disengaged joints incorporate the shoulders, fingers, and knees.
Preventive measures include reinforcing the muscles around the joints to give better strength. Competitors ought to utilize legitimate defensive stuff, and mentors ought to teach competitors on methods to safeguard weak joints during play. Speedy and fitting clinical consideration is fundamental in overseeing disengagements to limit long haul results.

9. **Stress Breaks:**
Stress breaks, small breaks in bones coming about because of dull pressure, frequently happen in weight-bearing bones like the shins and feet. Sports that include running and bouncing, for example, olympic style events or ball, represent a higher gamble for pressure cracks.
Preventive measures remember continuous movement for preparing power, appropriate footwear, and consolidating low-influence exercises to decrease the general weight on bones. Competitors ought to be instructed about the significance of appropriate sustenance, including adequate calcium and vitamin D, to help bone wellbeing and lessen the gamble of pressure cracks.

10. **Wounds and Injuries:**

While by and large less extreme, wounds (wounds) are normal in physical games or exercises with a gamble of effect, like hand to hand fighting or rugby. While not orthopedically complex, injuries can in any case cause agony and uneasiness, affecting a competitor's capacity to perform.

5.2 Emotional Impact of Sports Injuries

The Profound Effect of Sports Wounds: Exploring the Tempestuous Waters of Mental Difficulties

Taking part in sports is an excursion set apart by actual effort, collaboration, and the quest for greatness. Nonetheless, this excursion isn't without its portion of difficulties, and one of the most significant is the close to home effect of sports wounds. Wounds act actual mishaps like well as caused serious qualms about the psychological and profound prosperity of competitors. This investigation digs into the unpredictable profound scene that competitors explore when confronted with sports wounds, featuring the mental difficulties, survival techniques, and the significance of all encompassing help.

1. **Character and Self-esteem:**
   For some competitors, their game isn't simply a movement; it's a huge piece of their character. At the point when a physical issue sidelines them, it can prompt a significant feeling of misfortune and a scrutinizing of self-esteem. Competitors might wrestle with deep-seated insecurities, particularly in the event that their feeling of character is intently attached to their presentation and accomplishments in their game.

   Adapting to this close to home effect requires a change in context. Mentors, partners, and encouraging groups of people assume a significant part in stressing the diverse idea of a competitor's personality. Empowering competitors to investigate different parts of their characters, interests, and abilities helps in relieving the effect of a brief break from their game.

2. **Apprehension about the Unexplored world:**
   Sports wounds present a component of vulnerability, and the feeling of dread toward the obscure can be a critical wellspring of uneasiness for competitors. Inquiries concerning the degree of the injury, the span of recuperation, and whether they will get back to their pre-physical issue level of execution pose a potential threat. This dread can be deadening, influencing the recuperation interaction as well as the competitor's psychological prosperity.

   Building close to home flexibility includes tending to this dread head-on. Transparent correspondence from medical services experts about the injury, the normal recuperation course of events, and the means engaged with restoration helps in demystifying the unexplored world. Laying out reasonable assumptions and achievements helps competitors in recovering a feeling of control and reason.

3. **Profound Rollercoaster:**

The profound excursion following a games injury is frequently compared to a rollercoaster. Competitors might encounter a scope of feelings, from forswearing and outrage to pity and disappointment. The underlying shock of the injury, combined with the sudden interruption of their daily practice, can give approach to influxes of close to home choppiness surprisingly terms with the truth of their circumstance.

Giving a place of refuge to competitors to communicate their feelings is fundamental. Mentors, colleagues, and psychological wellness experts assume key parts in offering backing and understanding during this rollercoaster of feelings. Recognizing that these sentiments are a characteristic piece of the mending system assists competitors with exploring the close to home promising and less promising times.

4. **Separation and Distance:**

Sports wounds can prompt a feeling of separation and distance, particularly in group activities where brotherhood is a critical part. Competitors might feel disengaged from their colleagues, mentors, and the more extensive games local area. This detachment can strengthen sensations of depression and add to the personal difficulties they face.

Cultivating a feeling of having a place is pivotal in relieving the effect of detachment. Colleagues and mentors can keep up with ordinary correspondence, guaranteeing that the harmed competitor stays an esteemed piece of the group. Inclusivity measures, for example, including the harmed competitor in group exercises, keep a feeling of association and assist with easing sensations of estrangement.

5. **Loss of Certainty:**

Certainty is a delicate part of a competitor's mind, and a games injury can bargain a huge catastrophe for it. The feeling of dread toward not having the option to perform at similar level, worries about reinjury, and questions around one's capacities can dissolve a competitor's certainty. Modifying this certainty turns into a basic part of the recuperation cycle.

Steady movement in restoration, joined by little triumphs and accomplishments, adds to modifying certainty. Mentors assume a significant part in imparting conviction and stressing the competitor's assets. Putting forth sensible objectives and commending achievements en route assist in reestablishing certainty with venturing by step.

6. **Fretfulness and Dissatisfaction:**

Competitors are frequently adapted to stretch their actual boundaries, and the constrained restriction during injury recuperation can prompt anxiety and dissatisfaction. The powerlessness to take part in the exercises they love, combined with the apparent sluggish speed of recuperation, strengthens these feelings. Competitors might wrestle with a feeling of feebleness as they anticipate approval to completely continue their game.

Adapting to eagerness includes a change in center from prompt results to the course of recuperation. Teaching competitors about the significance of tolerance, slow advancement, and the job of rest in mending oversees dissatisfaction. Psychological wellness experts can help competitors in creating survival methods to explore the personal difficulties related with eagerness.

7. **Influence on Psychological wellness:**

The profound effect of sports wounds reaches out past brief misery; it can essentially affect a competitor's psychological well-being. Uneasiness and sorrow are normal colleagues during the recuperation interaction. The anxiety toward not having the option to get back to the game, worries about losing grants or vocation open doors, and the industrious vulnerability can negatively affect a competitor's psychological prosperity.

All encompassing psychological wellness support is foremost during this period. Customary registrations with emotional well-being experts, peer support gatherings, and mindfulness crusades on emotional wellness add to a steady climate. Perceiving the indications of emotional wellness challenges and interceding early can forestall the acceleration of issues.

8. **Survival strategies:**

Adapting to the close to home effect of sports wounds includes the turn of events and use of successful survival strategies. Competitors might profit from different techniques, including:

Representation and Symbolism: Utilizing mental symbolism to envision the recuperation cycle, effective exhibitions, and the possible re-visitation of game can cultivate a positive outlook.

Care and Contemplation: Integrating care practices and reflection into the everyday schedule assists in dealing with focusing, nervousness, and nosy considerations connected with the injury.

Objective Setting: Laying out practical present moment and long haul objectives gives a feeling of motivation and heading during the recuperation venture.

Social Help: Building and keeping areas of strength for an organization, including partners, mentors, companions, and family, guarantees that the competitor doesn't explore the inner difficulties alone.

Positive Self-Talk: Developing a propensity for positive self-talk balances negative contemplations and supports a useful mentality.

9. **The Job of Encouraging groups of people:**

Competitors don't get through the close to home effect of sports wounds in separation; their encouraging groups of people assume an essential part in their capacity to explore these difficulties. Mentors, partners, companions, family, and medical care experts structure an aggregate emotionally supportive network that gives consolation, sympathy, and reasonable help.

Mentors, specifically, have an obligation to establish a climate where competitors feel open to examining their feelings and looking for help. Advancing open correspondence, offering adaptability in preparing plans, and recognizing the close to home parts of the recuperation cycle add to a steady training approach.

10. **Returning More grounded:**

The close to home effect of sports wounds is without a doubt testing, however it is likewise a chance for development and versatility. Competitors who explore these personal difficulties with help, self-empathy, and powerful survival techniques frequently rise out of the involvement in freshly discovered strength. Getting back to don more grounded, both truly and intellectually, turns into a demonstration of their versatility and assurance.

5.3 Balancing Recovery and Mental Health

Adjusting Recuperation and Psychological well-being: Sustaining the Brain Body Association in the Mending System

The excursion of recuperating from wounds, especially in the domain of sports, stretches out past actual recovery. It unpredictably winds around together the domains of recuperation and psychological wellness, underlining the interconnectedness of the brain and body in the mending system. This investigation dives into the significance of finding some kind of harmony between actual recuperation and mental prosperity, perceiving the cooperative relationship that adds to a comprehensive and economical mending venture.

1. **The Brain Body Association:**
   The brain body association is a primary standard in the domain of wellbeing and health. It recognizes the unpredictable exchange among mental and actual prosperity, perceiving that one essentially impacts the other. With regards to injury recuperation, this association turns out to be especially notable as the psychological condition of an individual can affect the direction and adequacy of the actual mending process.

   Understanding the psyche body association includes recognizing that psychological well-being impacts actual wellbeing as well as the other way around. Profound prosperity can either work with or block the recuperation cycle. Positive mental states, like hopefulness and flexibility, have been connected to upgraded actual recuperation results, while stress, tension, and despondency can obstruct progress.

2. **Psychosocial Elements in Recuperation:**
   Past the physiological parts of recuperation, psychosocial factors assume an

essential part in forming a singular's reaction to injury. Social help, survival techniques, and the view of command over the recuperation cycle add to the psychosocial scene. Competitors, specifically, may confront extraordinary difficulties as their personalities are frequently intently attached to their actual capacities and execution.

The emotionally supportive network encompassing an individual can essentially affect their psychological wellness during recuperation. Mentors, partners, companions, and family assume essential parts in giving consolation, compassion, and functional help. Establishing a climate that cultivates a feeling of having a place and addresses psychosocial factors adds to a stronger and good recuperation experience.

3. **Adapting to Vulnerability:**

   In the domain of injury recuperation, vulnerability is a dependable friend. The dubious timetable of recuperation, the capriciousness of misfortunes, and the uncertainty encompassing the getting back to typical exercises can prompt pressure and nervousness. Adapting to this vulnerability requires versatile techniques that develop flexibility and a positive outlook.

   Competitors benefit from developing an outlook that embraces the excursion of recuperation as an opportunity for growth. Setting practical assumptions, separating the recuperation interaction into reasonable advances, and celebrating little triumphs en route give a feeling of control and inspiration. Care rehearses, like contemplation and profound breathing activities, can likewise be significant devices in exploring the vulnerabilities of recuperation.

4. **Tending to Psychological wellness Difficulties:**

   Emotional well-being difficulties, like uneasiness and melancholy, are normal during the recuperation stage. The profound effect of the injury, combined with the disturbances to one's daily schedule and way of life, can add to a decrease in mental prosperity. Distinguishing and tending to these difficulties right off the bat is principal for a complete way to deal with recuperation.

   Incorporating psychological well-being support into the general recuperation plan is fundamental. Competitors ought to approach emotional well-being experts who represent considerable authority in sports brain science and injury restoration. Normal registrations, guiding meetings, and the improvement of survival methods custom-made to the singular's requirements add to a proactive and steady way to deal with emotional wellness.

5. **All encompassing Restoration Projects:**

   Comprehensive restoration programs perceive that viable recuperation includes both physical and mental aspects. These projects go past conventional non-intrusive treatment and consolidate components that address the psychosocial parts of mending.

   Fitting restoration to the singular's necessities, objectives, and psychological well-being contemplations guarantees a more exhaustive and customized approach.

All encompassing restoration might incorporate components, for example, care preparing, stress the executives strategies, and objective setting works out. Mentors and medical services experts team up to establish a climate that sustains both the physical and mental prosperity of the person. This integrative methodology perceives that emotional wellness is certainly not a different substance however a necessary piece of the general mending process.

6. **Enabling Competitors:**

Enabling competitors during the recuperation interaction includes cultivating a feeling of organization and independence. Competitors who feel effectively engaged with their recuperation, pursue informed choices, and have a voice in their recovery plan are bound to encounter good emotional wellness results. Strengthening stretches out past the actual parts of recuperation to envelop dynamic cooperation in direction and objective setting.

Mentors, coaches, and medical services experts can enable competitors by including them in the arranging system, making sense of the reasoning behind unambiguous mediations, and requesting their contribution on objectives and achievements. This cooperative methodology not just upgrades the viability of the restoration plan yet in addition adds to a feeling of responsibility and control.

7. **Progressing Back to Game:**

The progress back to don addresses a vital stage in the recuperation excursion, and it requests cautious thought of both actual status and mental readiness. Competitors might wrestle with execution tension, apprehension about reinjury, and the strain to live up to assumptions. This progress requires an all encompassing methodology that tends to the mental difficulties related with getting back to cutthroat play.

Mentors assume a critical part in supporting competitors during this stage. Open correspondence, sensible objective setting, and slow movement in preparing and rivalry add to a smoother change. Psychological well-being experts can help competitors in creating survival methods for overseeing execution related pressure and nervousness, guaranteeing a balanced and reasonable re-visitation of game.

8. **Gaining from Mishaps:**

Mishaps are an intrinsic piece of the recuperation excursion, and what people answer difficulties significantly means for their psychological wellness. Competitors might encounter dissatisfaction, frustration, and a feeling of relapse when confronted with difficulties or defers in recuperation. Gaining from misfortunes includes developing versatility, flexibility, and a development mentality.

Mentors and encouraging groups of people can direct competitors in reevaluating difficulties as any open doors for learning and development. Empowering an inspirational perspective, underlining the headway made in spite of difficulties, and offering progressing help add to a strong mentality. Competitors who view misfortunes as transitory obstacles instead of unfavorable snags are better prepared to explore the personal difficulties of recuperation.

9. **Long haul Prosperity:**

The crossing point of recuperation and emotional well-being reaches out past the quick mending interaction to include long haul prosperity. Competitors who focus on their psychological well-being during recuperation are bound to encounter supported physical and close to home wellbeing soon after the injury. Long haul prosperity includes developing propensities and systems that add to progressing mental strength and positive actual results.

Integrating psychological wellness rehearses into the day to day daily schedule, keeping a reasonable way of life, and looking for help when required are indispensable parts of long haul prosperity. Competitors, mentors, and encouraging groups of people assume cooperative parts in cultivating a climate that focuses on the comprehensive wellbeing of people past the recuperation stage.

10. **The Job of Mentors and Encouraging groups of people:**

Mentors and encouraging groups of people hold critical impact in molding the recuperation experience for competitors. Mentors, specifically, assume diverse parts as guides, instructors, and inspirations. Establishing a climate that values emotional wellness, underlines open correspondence, and coordinates mental prosperity into the instructing reasoning adds to a positive and steady structure.

5.4 Preventive Measures and Mind-Body Connection

Preventive Measures and Psyche Body Association: A Comprehensive Way to deal with Injury Counteraction and Health

In the powerful domain of sports and proactive tasks, the quest for preventive measures is significant for deflecting wounds as well as for sustaining the psyche body association. This investigation digs into the diverse scene of preventive measures, accentuating the advantageous connection between actual wellbeing and mental prosperity. By embracing a comprehensive methodology that interlaces the two aspects, competitors might not just decrease the gamble of wounds at any point yet in addition improve their general health and execution.

1. **Actual Readiness and Molding:**

At the center of injury anticipation is actual readiness and molding. Competitors who focus on strength, adaptability, and cardiovascular wellness make a hearty groundwork that braces the body against possible wounds.

Molding programs custom fitted to the particular requests of the game add to improved biomechanics, lessening the gamble of strains, injuries, and abuse wounds.

The psyche body association becomes possibly the most important factor as competitors participate in deliberate and careful preparation. Coordinating care rehearses into molding schedules upgrades body mindfulness, permitting competitors to recognize and address uneven characters or compensatory developments that might add to injury risk. The development of a careful way to deal with actual readiness adjusts the psychological and actual parts of preparing, encouraging a far reaching way to deal with injury counteraction.

2. **Legitimate Warm-up and Chill off Schedules:**

The significance of legitimate warm-up and chill off schedules couldn't possibly be more significant in injury avoidance. A very much planned warm-up readies the body for the requests of active work by expanding blood stream, adaptability, and joint versatility. On the other hand, an exhaustive cool-down helps with muscle recuperation, diminishes muscle irritation, and advances adaptability, laying the basis for the following instructional course.

The psyche body association in warm-up and chill off schedules includes deliberate spotlight on the current second. Competitors rehearsing care during these stages improve actual planning as well as make a psychological space for focus and status. Careful development and extending add to further developed body mindfulness, permitting competitors to distinguish likely issues before they grow into wounds.

3. **Biomechanical Investigation and Procedure Refinement:**

Biomechanical examination assumes a pivotal part in physical issue counteraction by distinguishing defective development examples or procedures that might add to the gamble of wounds. Mentors and sports experts can direct point by point appraisals to pinpoint areas of concern and work cooperatively with competitors to refine their methods. Addressing biomechanical failures adds to ideal execution and decreases the probability of abuse wounds.

The psyche body association is obvious during the time spent method refinement. Competitors participated in careful work on, zeroing in on the subtleties of their developments, can deliberately address biomechanical imperfections. By adjusting mental attention to actual changes, competitors improve their specialized capability as well as add to injury avoidance by cultivating productive and controlled developments.

4. **Sustenance and Hydration:**

Sustenance and hydration are basic mainstays of athletic execution and injury counteraction. An even and supplement rich eating regimen upholds ideal actual capability, giving the body the fundamental components for muscle fix, energy creation, and in general prosperity. Hydration is similarly essential, as appropriate liquid admission guarantees satisfactory oil of joints and works with thermoregulation.

The psyche body association in nourishment lies in the attention to the effect of dietary decisions on both physical and mental states. Competitors who focus on sustenance are energizing their bodies for execution as well as affecting mental capabilities and mental flexibility. Careful eating rehearses, like focusing on craving and completion prompts, add to an all encompassing methodology that supports both the body and psyche.

5. **Rest and Recuperation Methodologies:**

Rest and recuperation are fundamental parts of injury anticipation, permitting the body to fix and adjust to the anxieties of preparing. Competitors who focus on adequate rest, dynamic recuperation methods, and rest days inside their preparation plans advance generally wellbeing. Legitimate recuperation procedures add to diminished weariness, worked on resistant capability, and improved mental concentration.

The psyche body association in rest and recuperation includes recognizing the significance of mental revival close by actual recovery. Competitors rehearsing care or unwinding strategies during recuperation periods add to pressure decrease and mental prosperity. Perceiving the interconnected idea of rest and psychological well-being cultivates a far reaching way to deal with injury counteraction that stretches out past the actual domain.

6. **Stress The executives and Mental Flexibility:**

Stress is a critical variable that can think twice about physical and mental prosperity, expanding the helplessness to wounds. Executing pressure the executives methods, like care, contemplation, and profound breathing activities, adds to mental strength. Competitors who develop a strong mentality are better prepared to explore the tensions of preparing, contest, and the innate vulnerabilities of sports.

The psyche body association in pressure the board is apparent in the physiological reactions to unwinding strategies. Practices, for example, care lighten mental pressure as well as trigger actual reactions, for example, diminished pulse and cortisol levels. Incorporating pressure the board into injury avoidance programs highlights the indistinguishable connection among mental and actual wellbeing.

7. **Broadly educating and Periodization:**

Broadly educating and periodization are methodologies that differentiate preparing schedules, relieving the gamble of abuse wounds and upgrading generally wellness. Broadly educating includes integrating various exercises into the preparation routine, decreasing the monotonous weights on unambiguous muscles or joints. Periodization includes orderly varieties in preparing power and volume to streamline execution and forestall burnout.

The psyche body association in broadly educating and periodization lies in the psychological versatility encouraged by fluctuated schedules. Competitors participated in assorted exercises challenge their bodies as well as animate mental commitment.

The psychological newness got from assortment adds to supported inspiration and lessens the psychological exhaustion related with repetitive preparation.

8. **Ordinary Checking and Screening:**

Ordinary checking and screening empower early recognition of expected issues, considering proactive mediation before wounds happen. Competitors going through intermittent appraisals, including biomechanical screenings, strength evaluations, and clinical assessments, make an establishment for customized injury counteraction procedures. Distinguishing and addressing risk factors in their beginning phases adds to long haul outer muscle wellbeing.

The brain body association in checking and screening includes elevated consciousness of one's actual state. Competitors effectively took part in self-evaluation and normal registrations with medical care experts foster a more profound comprehension of their bodies. This mindfulness stretches out to mental prosperity, making a comprehensive way to deal with checking that thinks about both physical and mental aspects.

9. **Instructive Drives:**

Instructive drives are instrumental in engaging competitors with information about injury anticipation, health rehearses, and the significance of the brain body association. Mentors, sports experts, and medical care suppliers can offer studios, assets, and customized direction to competitors. Taught competitors are bound to embrace preventive measures and participate in rehearses that advance in general prosperity.

The psyche body association in instructive drives includes encouraging a feeling of obligation and organization. Competitors who comprehend the reasoning behind preventive measures are bound to move toward their preparation and way of life decisions with care. Enabling competitors with information adds to a culture of comprehensive health inside the games local area.

10. **Developing a Positive Group Culture:**

Group culture assumes a urgent part in physical issue counteraction, impacting the aggregate mentality and ways of behaving of competitors. Groups that focus on correspondence, support, and a positive air establish a climate helpful for both physical and mental prosperity. A feeling of kinship cultivates open exchange about wounds, urges adherence to preventive measures, and elevates a common obligation to by and large wellbeing.

Chapter 6

Growing Pains: Orthopedic Considerations

Developing Agonies: Muscular Contemplations in Juvenile Turn of events

Youthfulness, set apart by fast actual development and hormonal changes, is a powerful period of life where the body goes through huge changes. While this time of development is fundamental for the improvement of a sound and versatile outer muscle framework, it likewise achieves muscular contemplations that merit consideration. This investigation dives into the complexities of developing torments, both physical and profound, and the muscular contemplations that assume an essential part in forming the outer muscle wellbeing of teenagers.

1. **Outer muscle Improvement during Youthfulness:**

   Youth is portrayed by an articulated development spray, where the body goes through sped up improvement as far as level, bulk, and bone thickness. The outer muscle framework, involving bones, muscles, tendons, and joints, encounters dynamic changes to oblige the requests of actual development.

   While this period is fundamental for accomplishing top bone mass and generally outer muscle strength, it additionally presents weaknesses that require cautious thought.

   The psyche body association in outer muscle advancement during immaturity is obvious in the exchange between actual development and profound prosperity. Teenagers encountering development sprays might wrestle with both the energy and difficulties of these changes, featuring the significance of a comprehensive way to deal with muscular contemplations that tends to both physical and close to home aspects.

2. **Development Related Muscular Circumstances:**

   The quick development during youth can lead to explicit muscular circumstances that influence the creating outer muscle framework. Conditions like Osgood-Schlatter infection, Cut off's illness, and Scoliosis are instances of development related muscular difficulties. Osgood-Schlatter illness, portrayed by irritation of the patellar tendon, frequently appears during the young adult development spray, especially in people engaged with sports.

Cut off's illness, an aggravation of the development plate in the heel, is one more condition connected to the fast development of bones during pre-adulthood, frequently influencing youthful competitors. Scoliosis, a horizontal shape of the spine, may turn out to be more articulated during development sprays. These circumstances highlight the significance of watchful muscular consideration that considers the remarkable difficulties presented by the powerful development stage.

3. **Biomechanical Transformations:**

As the body goes through development and improvement, biomechanical transformations happen to keep up with equilibrium and usefulness. Changes in appendage length, muscle strength, and joint arrangement might affect biomechanics, impacting step, stance, and in general development designs. These biomechanical transformations are fundamental for obliging the developing body, yet they additionally present contemplations for muscular wellbeing.

The psyche body association in biomechanical transformations lies in the familiarity with these progressions and their likely effect on actual prosperity. Youths who comprehend the biomechanical shifts happening in their bodies can effectively participate in exercises that help solid outer muscle improvement. This mindfulness encourages a feeling of organization and obligation regarding one's muscular wellbeing.

4. **Active work and Muscular Wellbeing:**

Actual work is a foundation of juvenile turn of events, adding to the strength, adaptability, and generally wellbeing of the outer muscle framework. In any case, finding some kind of harmony between participating in normal actual work and it is pivotal to forestall abuse wounds.

Youths engaged with sports or incredible proactive tasks ought to be aware of their preparation power, appropriate warm-up and chill off schedules, and the significance of rest and recuperation.

The brain body association in actual work and muscular wellbeing includes perceiving the profound parts of commitment in sports. Young people frequently determine euphoria, brotherhood, and a feeling of character from their support in proactive tasks. Coordinating profound prosperity into muscular contemplations elevates an extensive way to deal with outer muscle wellbeing that recognizes the indistinguishable connection among physical and close to home aspects.

5. **Nourishment and Bone Wellbeing:**

Sufficient nourishment assumes an essential part in supporting bone wellbeing during puberty. The expanded interest for calcium, vitamin D, and different supplements fundamental for bone improvement highlights the significance of a fair eating routine. Legitimate sustenance not just backings the development of solid and thick bones yet additionally adds to the anticipation of conditions like osteoporosis further down the road.

The psyche body association in nourishment and bone wellbeing is apparent in the effect of dietary decisions on both physical and profound prosperity. Young people who focus on sustenance are putting resources into their outer muscle wellbeing as well as impacting mental capabilities and mental flexibility. The interaction among nourishment and close to home prosperity features the requirement for an all encompassing way to deal with muscular contemplations that tends to the two aspects.

6. **Injury Anticipation and Recovery:**

Teenagers participated in proactive tasks are defenseless to wounds, going from injuries and strains to additional complex muscular issues. Injury avoidance systems, including legitimate warm-up schedules, steady movement in preparing, and the utilization of defensive stuff, are foremost. In case of wounds, convenient and far reaching restoration is essential for a full recuperation and the counteraction of long haul outer muscle issues.

The brain body association in injury counteraction and restoration includes the mental parts of strength and adapting. Young people confronting wounds might encounter inner difficulties connected with mishaps, apprehension about re-injury, and the disappointment of hindered proactive tasks. Incorporating emotional well-being support into muscular consideration recognizes the all encompassing nature of prosperity and elevates a thorough way to deal with juvenile outer muscle wellbeing.

7. **Postural Propensities and Ergonomics:**

The improvement of postural propensities during puberty can lastingly affect outer muscle wellbeing.

As teenagers invest huge energy participated in stationary exercises, for example, considering and utilizing electronic gadgets, thoughtfulness regarding ergonomics becomes fundamental. Keeping up with legitimate stance, integrating breaks for development, and making ergonomic work areas add to the anticipation of muscular issues.

The psyche body association in postural propensities and ergonomics includes the attention to what stance means for profound states. Unfortunate stance can add to inconvenience, weakness, and even sensations of stress. Teenagers who effectively take part in rehearses that advance great stance are supporting their outer muscle wellbeing as well as cultivating profound prosperity.

8. **Profound Prosperity and Muscular Wellbeing:**

The profound prosperity of youths is complicatedly connected to their muscular wellbeing. The difficulties presented by development related muscular circumstances, biomechanical transformations, and wounds can have profound consequences. Youths encountering torment or actual restrictions might wrestle with disappointment, tension, or a feeling of disengagement from exercises they appreciate.

The brain body association in close to home prosperity and muscular wellbeing includes perceiving and tending to the profound parts of outer muscle difficulties. Coordinating psychological well-being support into muscular consideration recognizes the interconnected idea of physical and close to home prosperity. Youths who get all encompassing consideration that considers the two aspects are better prepared to explore the intricacies of muscular wellbeing during this groundbreaking period of life.

6.1 Ortho Challenges Related to Growth Spurts

Muscular Difficulties Connected with Development Sprays: Exploring the Pinnacles and Valleys of Young adult Turn of events

The juvenile years, set apart by the beginning of pubescence and fast development sprays, are an extraordinary stage that shapes both the physical and close to home scene of people. As the body goes through massive changes to accomplish its grown-up structure, a large group of muscular difficulties arises, requesting consideration and cautious route. This investigation digs into the complexities of muscular difficulties connected with development sprays, revealing insight into the pinnacles and valleys that portray this basic time of outer muscle improvement.

1. **The Elements of Development Sprays:**
   Development sprays, energized by hormonal changes, mean a time of sped up actual improvement during youth. Bones stretch, muscles fortify, and the in general outer muscle framework goes through significant changes to oblige the thriving body. While development sprays are fundamental for accomplishing top bone mass and outer muscle strength, they likewise present a bunch of difficulties that can influence muscular wellbeing.

   The psyche body association in the elements of development sprays is clear in the exchange between actual changes and close to home prosperity. Teenagers encountering quick development might wrestle with both the fervor and difficulties presented by these changes. The consciousness of this unpredictable association frames the establishment for an all encompassing way to deal with muscular difficulties during development sprays.

2. **Osgood-Schlatter Infection:**
   Osgood-Schlatter sickness, a typical muscular condition during youth, appears as irritation of the patellar tendon, just beneath the kneecap. This condition is especially pervasive among young people participated in sports or exercises that include continuous running and bouncing. The quick development of bones,

joined with the pressure put on the patellar tendon, adds to the improvement of Osgood-Schlatter infection.

The psyche body association in Osgood-Schlatter illness includes the close to home effect of agony and actual impediments. Teenagers encountering this condition might battle with disappointment, particularly assuming that it obstructs their support in sports or proactive tasks they appreciate. A thorough way to deal with Osgood-Schlatter sickness tends to both the actual parts of irritation and the close to home prosperity of the person.

3. **Cut off's Illness:**

Cut off's illness, otherwise called calcaneal apophysitis, is another development related muscular test that influences the heel. It includes irritation of the development plate in the heel, frequently happening during the young adult development spray. This condition is common among youthful competitors, especially those engaged with exercises that include dull effect on the heels, like running or bouncing.

The psyche body association in Cut off's illness spins around the profound experience of torment and distress. Teenagers with Cut off's illness might wrestle with constraints in their capacity to participate in proactive tasks, affecting their close to home prosperity. Muscular consideration that considers both the actual treatment of irritation and the basic reassurance of the individual adds to a more all encompassing methodology.

4. **Scoliosis:**

Scoliosis, a parallel curve of the spine, may turn out to be more articulated during development sprays. While some level of arch is typical, exorbitant or unusual spinal curve can present muscular difficulties. The unique changes in the outer muscle framework during development sprays, combined with hereditary variables, add to the turn of events or compounding of scoliosis in certain teenagers.

The psyche body association in scoliosis includes the profound effect of a noticeable and some of the time moderate condition.

Youths with scoliosis might encounter reluctance or self-perception concerns, particularly during a period of life where peer discernments assume a critical part. Muscular consideration for scoliosis shouldn't just zero in on the actual administration of bend yet in addition address the close to home prosperity of the person.

5. **Biomechanical Variations:**

The quick development and lengthening of bones during puberty lead to biomechanical variations to keep up with equilibrium and usefulness. Changes in appendage length, muscle strength, and joint arrangement might affect biomechanics, impacting walk, stance, and generally speaking development designs. While these variations are fundamental for obliging the developing body, they can likewise present difficulties that influence muscular wellbeing.

The brain body association in biomechanical transformations lies in the attention to these progressions and their expected effect on actual prosperity. Youths who comprehend the biomechanical shifts happening in their bodies can effectively participate in exercises that help sound outer muscle advancement. This mindfulness encourages a feeling of organization and obligation regarding one's muscular wellbeing.

6. **Abuse Wounds:**

The excitement and energy of youthfulness frequently drive expanded support in sports and proactive tasks. While actual work is fundamental for generally wellbeing, the gamble of abuse wounds heightens during development sprays. Abuse wounds, for example, stress breaks, tendonitis, and tendon strains, can result from dreary weight on unambiguous bones or joints. The outer muscle framework, actually adjusting to fast development, might be more vulnerable to these wounds.

The psyche body association in abuse wounds includes the close to home part of mishaps and actual restrictions. Youths energetic about their association in sports might encounter dissatisfaction or frustration when confronted with abuse wounds that require rest and recovery. Muscular consideration ought to address the actual restoration as well as the profound prosperity of the individual exploring the difficulties of recuperation.

7. **Influence on Stance and Spinal Wellbeing:**

Development sprays can impact stance and spinal wellbeing, especially with regards to expanded screen time and stationary exercises. As teenagers invest more energy examining or utilizing electronic gadgets, keeping up with legitimate stance becomes significant. Unfortunate stance during development sprays might add to inconvenience, exhaustion, and, after some time, outer muscle issues like back agony and spinal misalignments.

The brain body association in stance and spinal wellbeing includes perceiving the close to home effect of distress and agony. Youths encountering back torment or postural difficulties might battle with pressure and a decreased personal satisfaction.

Muscular consideration that tends to both the actual parts of stance and the close to home prosperity of the singular backings a more thorough way to deal with spinal wellbeing.

8. **Preventive Measures and Training:**

Proactive muscular consideration during development sprays includes an emphasis on preventive measures and schooling. Teaching young people about the outer muscle transforms they are encountering, legitimate ergonomics, and the significance of adjusted actual work can engage them to play a functioning job in their muscular wellbeing. Preventive measures, including customary actual work, strength preparing, and adaptability works out, add to a versatile outer muscle framework.

The psyche body association in preventive measures and training bases on the strengthening of teenagers. Proficient people are bound to pursue informed decisions that help their muscular wellbeing and by and large prosperity. Muscular consideration that consolidates schooling and preventive techniques sustains a feeling of obligation for one's wellbeing, cultivating a proactive way to deal with outer muscle difficulties during development sprays.

6.2 Impact on Bones and Joints

Influence on Bones and Joints: Exploring the Muscular Territory of Young adult Development Sprays

Youth, a period of quick development and hormonal changes, introduces a powerful period where the outer muscle framework goes through significant changes. The effect on bones and joints during development sprays is a focal part of juvenile turn of events, introducing the two open doors for vigorous outer muscle wellbeing and difficulties that require insightful thought. This investigation digs into the complex exchange between development sprays and the outer muscle framework, analyzing the significant impacts on bones and joints and exploring the muscular landscape one of a kind to this groundbreaking stage.

1. **Bone Development and Improvement:**

    Development sprays during immaturity are portrayed by critical bone development and improvement. Long bones, for example, the femur and tibia, experience prolongation at the development plates, worked with by the activity of development chemicals. This period is urgent for achieving top bone mass, a determinant of skeletal strength and versatility in later life. Satisfactory bone thickness accomplished during pre-adulthood adds to diminished dangers of osteoporosis and breaks in adulthood.

    The brain body association in bone development and advancement lies in the familiarity with the double effect on physical and close to home prosperity. Young people encountering fast bone development might wind up adjusting to changes in level and height, affecting self-perception and self-discernment.

    An exhaustive way to deal with muscular consideration thinks about the physiological parts of bone improvement as well as the profound elements of mental self view during this extraordinary stage.

2. **Joint Variations and Arrangement:**

    Close by bone development, joints go through variations to oblige the progressions in appendage length and by and large outer muscle structure. Joint arrangement is urgent for keeping up with legitimate biomechanics and ideal usefulness. Development sprays can present varieties in joint arrangement, affecting walk, stance, and development designs. While these transformations are fundamental for the developing body, they can present difficulties that influence muscular wellbeing.

The brain body association in joint transformations and arrangement includes the cognizant attention to development and stance. Youths effectively participated in exercises that advance body mindfulness, like yoga or utilitarian activities, add to more readily joint arrangement. This mindfulness encourages a feeling of organization over one's outer muscle wellbeing and supports the improvement of solid development designs during the extraordinary time of development.

3. **Possible Muscular Difficulties:**

The quick development of bones and the relating variations in joints can lead to likely muscular difficulties. Conditions like Osgood-Schlatter illness and Cut off's sickness, described by aggravation close to the knee and heel, separately, are frequently connected with development sprays. Scoliosis, a sidelong bend of the spine, may turn out to be more articulated during this stage. These difficulties feature the requirement for watchful muscular consideration that tends to the extraordinary contemplations of the creating outer muscle framework.

The psyche body association in potential muscular difficulties includes the close to home effect of conditions that might restrict proactive tasks. Teenagers confronting muscular difficulties might encounter dissatisfaction, tension, or a feeling of limitation in their capacity to take part in sports or exercises they appreciate. A comprehensive muscular methodology considers the physiological administration of conditions as well as the close to home prosperity of the individual exploring these difficulties.

4. **Weight-Bearing Exercises and Bone Thickness:**

Weight-bearing exercises, like running, hopping, and obstruction preparing, assume a crucial part in bone wellbeing during development sprays. These exercises animate bone arrangement and improve bone thickness, adding to skeletal strength. The effect of weight-bearing exercises on bone thickness is especially critical during youthfulness, as this is a time of elevated bone renovating and transformation.

The brain body association in weight-bearing exercises and bone thickness includes the profound part of commitment in proactive tasks. Youths frequently determine bliss, kinship, and a feeling of character from their support in sports. The positive close to home encounters related with weight-bearing exercises add to an all encompassing way to deal with muscular consideration, perceiving the indistinguishable connection among physical and profound aspects.

5. **Joint Pressure and Abuse Wounds:**

While actual work is fundamental for bone wellbeing, the expanded interest on joints during development sprays can prompt joint pressure and abuse wounds. Abuse wounds, for example, stress cracks, tendonitis, or tendon strains, may happen when the requests on joints surpass their ability for variation. The weakness of joints during development sprays underlines the significance of a fair way to deal with active work.

The psyche body association in joint pressure and abuse wounds includes the close to home reaction to misfortunes and actual constraints. Young people energetic about their contribution in sports might encounter dissatisfaction or disillusionment when confronted with abuse wounds that require rest and recovery. Muscular consideration ought to address the actual restoration as well as the profound prosperity of the individual exploring the difficulties of recuperation.

6. **Nourishment and Muscular Wellbeing:**

Sufficient sustenance is a foundation of muscular wellbeing during development sprays. The expanded interest for calcium, vitamin D, and different supplements fundamental for bone improvement highlights the significance of a fair eating regimen. Appropriate sustenance not just backings the development of solid and thick bones yet additionally adds to the counteraction of conditions like osteoporosis further down the road.

The psyche body association in nourishment and muscular wellbeing is obvious in the effect of dietary decisions on both physical and profound prosperity. Teenagers who focus on sustenance are putting resources into their outer muscle wellbeing as well as impacting mental capabilities and mental strength. The transaction among nourishment and profound prosperity features the requirement for an all encompassing way to deal with muscular contemplations that tends to the two aspects.

7. **Mental Effect of Muscular Contemplations:**

The muscular contemplations during development sprays can mentally affect youths. Conditions like scoliosis or muscular difficulties that limit proactive tasks might impact confidence and self-perception. The close to home reaction to these contemplations highlights the requirement for a thorough methodology that recognizes the interconnected idea of physical and profound prosperity.

The brain body association in the mental effect of muscular contemplations includes perceiving and tending to the profound parts of outer muscle difficulties. Coordinating psychological well-being support into muscular consideration recognizes the all encompassing nature of prosperity and elevates an extensive way to deal with juvenile outer muscle wellbeing. Teenagers who get comprehensive consideration that considers the two aspects are better prepared to explore the intricacies of muscular wellbeing during this extraordinary period of life.

6.3 Emotional Response to Physical Changes

Close to home Reaction to Actual Changes: Exploring the Violent Waters of Juvenile Change

Immaturity, a period set apart by huge actual changes, isn't just a period of real change yet additionally an excursion through the mind boggling scene of feelings. The profound reaction to these actual changes is a nuanced and basic part of juvenile turn of events, molding self-discernment, social collaborations, and generally mental prosperity. This investigation digs into the complicated interchange between actual changes and the close to home domain during pre-adulthood, exploring the fierce waters of change and the significant effect on the person's close to home scene.

1. **Self-perception and Self-Discernment:**
   The actual changes that go with puberty, including development sprays, changes in body extents, and the improvement of auxiliary sexual qualities, can essentially impact self-perception and self-discernment. Young people might end up wrestling with the acclimation to a quickly changing actual appearance, frequently under the examination of cultural excellence norms. The close to home reaction to shifts in self-perception assumes a vital part in forming confidence and self-esteem.

   The psyche body association in self-perception and self-discernment includes the close to home translation of actual changes. Teenagers encountering these progressions might explore identity cognizance, correlation with peers, and an elevated consciousness of their bodies. A complete way to deal with close to home prosperity perceives the interconnected idea of physical and profound aspects, cultivating a positive and tolerating self-discernment during this groundbreaking stage.

2. **Social Correlation and Companion Impact:**
   The close to home reaction to actual changes is unpredictably attached to social elements and friend impact. Teenagers frequently participate in friendly examination, assessing their actual appearance comparable to their companions. The strain to adjust to cultural guidelines of excellence, sustained by media and social stages, can heighten the close to home effect of actual changes. The longing for social acknowledgment and the apprehension about judgment add to the complex profound scene of immaturity.

   The brain body association in friendly examination and companion impact includes the profound cost of looking for approval and acknowledgment. Teenagers might encounter nervousness about fitting in or adjusting to apparent standards, affecting their decisions and ways of behaving. Tending to the close to home parts of social examination requires cultivating flexibility, self-acknowledgment, and a sound comprehension of individual uniqueness inside the social texture.

3. **Character Arrangement and Self-Disclosure:**
   Actual changes during immaturity assume an essential part in the more extensive setting of character development and self-revelation. The arising feeling of

personality is firmly entwined with how people see themselves truly and how they accept others see them. The close to home reaction to actual changes turns into an impetus for self-investigation, adding to the many-sided course of framing a durable and true character.

The psyche body association in character development includes the close to home investigation of one's genuineness as a part of self-revelation. Young people exploring this territory might wrestle with inquiries of self-definition, individual qualities, and the arrangement of their actual appearance with their inner feeling of character. Sustaining a positive profound reaction to actual changes becomes basic to encouraging a versatile and bona fide identity.

4. **Close to home Rollercoaster of Hormonal Changes:**

Hormonal changes, a sign of puberty, add to the close to home rollercoaster experienced by people during this stage. Vacillations in chemicals, like estrogen and testosterone, impact temperament, profound responsiveness, and feelings of anxiety. The profound reaction to hormonal changes can appear as emotional episodes, peevishness, and elevated aversion to stressors.

The brain body association in the close to home rollercoaster of hormonal changes includes perceiving the physiological premise of profound reactions. Young people might profit from understanding the connection between hormonal variances and temperament shifts, working with a more merciful and informed way to deal with their close to home encounters. Incorporating the ability to appreciate anyone on a deeper level into training about hormonal changes engages teenagers to explore this part of their improvement with strength and mindfulness.

5. **Influence on Psychological wellness and Prosperity:**

The close to home reaction to actual changes can significantly affect psychological wellness and by and large prosperity. Young people exploring the difficulties of self-insight, social elements, and hormonal vacillations might be powerless against stress, nervousness, and even circumstances like sorrow. The unpredictable transaction between actual changes and emotional well-being highlights the requirement for an all encompassing methodology that tends to the two aspects. The psyche body association in the effect on psychological wellness includes perceiving the proportional connection between close to home prosperity and actual wellbeing. Youths encountering profound misery might show actual side effects, like changes in craving, rest aggravations, or exhaustion. On the other hand, focusing on psychological wellness through daily reassurance, survival methods, and taking care of oneself adds to a stronger reaction to the inner difficulties of actual changes.

6. **Parental and Grown-up Help:**

Close to home reactions to actual changes can be essentially affected by the help given by guardians and different grown-ups. Open correspondence, approval of sentiments, and a non-critical methodology establish a steady climate for young people exploring the intricacies of change. Grown-ups who recognize the close to home components of actual changes add to the generally speaking mental prosperity of young people.

The brain body association in parental and grown-up help includes perceiving the effect of profound approval on both mental and actual wellbeing. Teenagers who feel upheld in their profound reactions to actual changes are bound to foster sound survival strategies and an uplifting perspective. Cultivating a climate where profound articulation is urged adds to an all encompassing methodology that thinks about both the close to home and actual components of youth.

7. **Social and Cultural Impacts:**

Social and cultural impacts shape the profound scene of teenagers, affecting how they see their bodies and explore the assumptions put upon them. Social principles of magnificence, media portrayals, and cultural standards add to the close to home reaction to actual changes. Youths might incorporate these impacts, influencing their confidence and close to home prosperity.

The psyche body association in social and cultural impacts includes perceiving the outside factors that add to the close to home reactions of teenagers. Tending to these impacts requires encouraging decisive reasoning, media education, and a sound comprehension of different body types and articulations. A complete way to deal with profound prosperity recognizes the job of social and cultural elements in forming the close to home reaction to actual changes.

8. **Instructive Drives on Close to home Prosperity:**

Integrating instructive drives on close to home prosperity into school educational plans can engage youths with the devices to explore the inner difficulties of actual changes. Exhaustive sex training programs that remember conversations for close to home wellbeing, confidence, and ways of dealing with especially difficult times give significant assets to youths. Coordinating ability to appreciate individuals on a deeper level training cultivates versatility and mindfulness.

The psyche body association in instructive drives on profound prosperity includes perceiving the job of information in molding close to home reactions. Youths furnished with data about the physiological and profound parts of actual changes are more ready to explore this extraordinary stage. Training turns into an extension between understanding the brain body association and cultivating a positive close to home reaction to the intricacies of youthfulness.

6.4 Orthopedic Strategies for Growing Bodies

Muscular Methodologies for Developing Bodies: Sustaining Outer muscle Wellbeing in Youth

Immaturity, a powerful stage set apart by quick development and improvement, presents extraordinary difficulties and open doors for outer muscle wellbeing.

Muscular methodologies custom fitted to the particular necessities of developing bodies become foremost during this groundbreaking period. This investigation digs into the complex components of muscular consideration for young people, enveloping preventive measures, active work contemplations, and the advancement of by and large prosperity to sustain the outer muscle wellbeing of the thriving youth.

1. **Thorough Muscular Appraisals:**
   The underpinning of muscular techniques for developing bodies lies in exhaustive evaluations that think about the extraordinary necessities of young people. Standard outer muscle assessments, incorporating joint scope of movement, pose, and biomechanical evaluations, give important experiences into the person's muscular wellbeing. Recognizing any deviations or potential issues from the beginning empowers designated intercessions and preventive measures.
   The brain body association in exhaustive muscular appraisals includes the acknowledgment of what actual prosperity means for close to home states. Teenagers effectively participated in understanding their outer muscle wellbeing are bound to foster a feeling of organization and obligation, encouraging a good outlook towards their developing bodies.

2. **Individualized Exercise Solutions:**
   Active work is a foundation of muscular procedures for developing bodies. Notwithstanding, perceiving the uniqueness of youths is significant in creating exercise remedies. Fitting activities to oblige development sprays, biomechanical variations, and potential muscular difficulties guarantees that the actual work is both successful and safe. This individualized methodology adds to the improvement of a versatile and even outer muscle framework.
   The psyche body association in individualized practice remedies includes the profound experience of participating in proactive tasks.
   Young people who take part in practices that line up with their capacities and interests are bound to determine happiness, fulfillment, and a feeling of achievement. This positive close to home affiliation cultivates a deep rooted obligation to actual prosperity.

3. **Strength Preparing and Molding:**
   Integrating strength preparing and molding into muscular procedures for developing bodies is instrumental in supporting in general outer muscle wellbeing. Opposition practices focusing on significant muscle bunches improve bone thickness, joint dependability, and strong strength. Participating in age-proper strength preparing programs adds to injury avoidance, particularly in teenagers associated with sports or actually requesting exercises.
   The brain body association in strength preparing and molding includes the familiarity with actual strength as a wellspring of strengthening. Youths who

experience the positive effect of solidarity preparing may foster a versatile outer muscle framework as well as upgraded self-assurance and profound strength.

4. **Adaptability and Scope of Movement Activities:**
Underscoring adaptability and scope of movement practices is fundamental to muscular procedures for developing bodies. Dynamic extending schedules advance joint versatility and adaptability, decreasing the gamble of outer muscle wounds. Integrating these activities into the day to day schedule upholds the versatile idea of the outer muscle framework during pre-adulthood, forestalling solidness and advancing ideal development designs.

The psyche body association in adaptability practices includes the close to home insight of opportunity in development. Teenagers who develop adaptability and scope of movement are probably going to encounter a feeling of actual opportunity, decidedly influencing their close to home prosperity and generally speaking personal satisfaction.

5. **Act Mindfulness and Ergonomics:**
Muscular consideration for developing bodies remembers a concentration for act mindfulness and ergonomics, particularly taking into account the predominance of stationary exercises. Youths invest critical energy examining or utilizing electronic gadgets, making consideration regarding stance essential. Advancing great stance and instructing young people on ergonomics encourages outer muscle wellbeing, forestalling muscular issues connected with poor postural propensities.

The psyche body association in act mindfulness includes perceiving the profound effect of uneasiness and agony related with unfortunate stance. Youths who effectively participate in rehearses that advance great stance support their outer muscle wellbeing as well as experience profound prosperity through diminished actual distress.

6. **Dietary Help for Bone Wellbeing:**
An all encompassing way to deal with muscular techniques for developing bodies incorporates nourishing help, especially for bone wellbeing. Satisfactory admission of calcium, vitamin D, and other fundamental supplements upholds the improvement of solid and thick bones. Nourishment assumes a significant part in forestalling conditions like osteoporosis and supporting the outer muscle framework during the basic time of development.

The psyche body association in wholesome help includes perceiving the effect of dietary decisions on both physical and profound prosperity. Teenagers who focus on nourishment are putting resources into their outer muscle wellbeing as well as affecting mental capabilities and mental strength.

7. **Injury Avoidance Projects:**
Coordinating injury avoidance programs into muscular systems is principal for young people associated with sports or proactive tasks. These projects frequently

incorporate warm-up schedules, neuromuscular preparation, and instruction on legitimate methods. Preventive measures fundamentally add to decreasing the frequency of abuse wounds and horrendous muscular circumstances.

The psyche body association in injury avoidance programs includes the profound part of misfortunes and actual constraints. Young people energetic about their association in sports might encounter dissatisfaction or frustration when confronted with wounds. Muscular consideration ought to address the actual restoration as well as the close to home prosperity of the individual exploring the difficulties of recuperation.

8. **Psychosocial Backing and Emotional well-being Coordination:**
Perceiving the psychosocial parts of muscular consideration is significant for an all encompassing way to deal with developing bodies. Youths confronting muscular difficulties might encounter close to home misery connected with actual impediments, self-perception concerns, or disturbances in their standard exercises. Incorporating psychosocial support and emotional well-being assets into muscular consideration recognizes the interconnected idea of physical and close to home prosperity.

The brain body association in psychosocial support includes perceiving the profound effect of muscular difficulties on emotional well-being. Teenagers who get comprehensive consideration that considers the two aspects are better prepared to explore the intricacies of muscular wellbeing during this groundbreaking period of life.

9. **Instructive Drives for Taking care of oneself:**

Enabling young people with information about taking care of oneself is a crucial part of muscular systems for developing bodies. Instructive drives that emphasis on grasping outer muscle wellbeing, perceiving the indications of possible issues, and taking on taking care of oneself practices impart a feeling of obligation and dynamic commitment to one's prosperity.

The psyche body association in instructive drives for taking care of oneself includes perceiving the job of information in molding close to home reactions. Youths furnished with data about the physiological and profound parts of muscular wellbeing are more ready to explore this groundbreaking stage.

Chapter 7

Mental Health Support for Ortho Patients

Emotional well-being Backing for Muscular Patients: An All encompassing Way to deal with Recuperating

Muscular circumstances, whether intense wounds or ongoing outer muscle issues, not just effect the actual prosperity of patients yet in addition convey significant ramifications for their emotional well-being. Perceiving the unpredictable transaction among physical and mental prosperity is pivotal in giving exhaustive consideration to muscular patients. This investigation digs into the multi-layered elements of psychological wellness support for people exploring muscular difficulties, featuring the significance of an all encompassing way to deal with mending.

1. **Close to home Effect of Muscular Circumstances:**

   Muscular circumstances frequently achieve a scope of feelings for patients. The unexpected disturbance of portability, expected torment, and the vulnerability of recuperation can prompt sensations of disappointment, tension, and even sorrow.

   The close to home effect isn't restricted to the individual encountering the condition; it reaches out to relatives and parental figures who might partake in the profound excursion.

   The brain body association in the profound effect of muscular circumstances includes perceiving the equal connection among physical and emotional well-being. Tending to the profound prosperity of patients recognizes the interconnected idea of their encounters and adds to a more all encompassing way to deal with muscular consideration.

2. **Ongoing Agony and Emotional well-being:**

   Persistent torment, frequently connected with muscular circumstances, can negatively affect a person's emotional well-being. The constant idea of agony might prompt sensations of powerlessness, disappointment, and even add to the turn of events or compounding of tension and melancholy. Overseeing constant torment requires actual mediations as well as a thorough methodology that incorporates emotional well-being support.

The brain body association in constant torment and emotional wellness includes perceiving what profound prosperity means for the discernment and the executives of agony. Coordinating psychological well-being support into the consideration plan for muscular patients with persistent torment tends to the actual side effects as well as the close to home parts of their experience.

3. **Acclimation to Impediments and Way of life Changes:**
   Muscular circumstances frequently require way of life changes and changes, like impediments in portability, alterations in day to day exercises, or even the requirement for assistive gadgets. Changing in accordance with these progressions can be sincerely difficult, expecting people to adjust to another typical. This interaction includes actual recovery as well as basic reassurance to explore the mental parts of change.

   The psyche body association in acclimating to constraints includes understanding how profound flexibility adds to the general restoration process. Muscular consideration that incorporates psychological well-being support perceives the significance of assisting patients with adapting to the inner difficulties related with way of life changes, cultivating a positive outlook for variation.

4. **Influence on Freedom and Personality:**
   Muscular circumstances might affect a singular's feeling of freedom and character. Loss of versatility or capability can provoke one's capacity to perform day to day errands freely, prompting a feeling of reliance on others. Also, the change in jobs and capacities might impact how people see themselves, affecting their personality and confidence.

   The psyche body association in the effect on autonomy and personality includes perceiving the profound meaning of these changes. Psychological well-being support becomes fundamental in assisting people with exploring the close to home landscape of changing their self-discernment and rethinking parts of their character with regards to their muscular condition.

5. **Psychosocial Variables and Restoration Results:**
   Psychosocial factors assume a significant part in restoration results for muscular patients. Profound prosperity, social help, and mental strength are interconnected with the actual recovery process. People encountering positive psychosocial support are much of the time more propelled, participated in their recovery works out, and exhibit better adherence to treatment plans.

   The brain body association in psychosocial elements and restoration results includes perceiving the harmonious connection between psychological wellness and actual recuperation. Thorough muscular consideration incorporates tending to psychosocial factors, encouraging a steady climate that upgrades restoration results and in general prosperity.

6. **Correspondence and Patient Schooling:**
Open correspondence and patient schooling are major parts of emotional wellness support for muscular patients. Giving clear data about the condition, treatment choices, and the normal direction of recuperation enables people to partake in their consideration effectively. Straightforward correspondence likewise mitigates tension and vulnerability, adding to a positive mental state.

The psyche body association in correspondence and patient schooling includes perceiving the effect of information on profound prosperity. Very much educated patients are better prepared to deal with the inner difficulties of their muscular circumstances, cultivating a feeling of control and understanding that decidedly impacts their emotional well-being.

7. **Cooperative Consideration:**
Cooperative consideration models that include a multidisciplinary group are progressively perceived as the need might arise of muscular patients. Muscular specialists, actual advisors, torment subject matter experts, and emotional wellness experts team up to give thorough consideration. This incorporated methodology considers the physical, profound, and mental parts of the patient's insight.

The brain body association in cooperative consideration includes perceiving that tending to psychological well-being isn't an independent part of care however a fundamental piece of the general patient excursion. Cooperative consideration models improve the viability of muscular mediations by recognizing and tending to the interconnected idea of physical and mental prosperity.

8. **Survival techniques and Flexibility Building:**
Psychological wellness support for muscular patients incorporates the advancement of ways of dealing with hardship or stress and strength building strategies. Showing people how to oversee pressure, adapt to torment, and develop close to home strength furnishes them with instruments to explore the difficulties of their muscular excursion. Incorporating these methodologies into the consideration plan improves the singular's capacity to adapt to both physical and profound parts of their condition.

The psyche body association in survival methods includes perceiving that close to home strength emphatically impacts the view of agony and the capacity to stick to restoration plans. Muscular consideration that consolidates flexibility building methodologies cultivates an outlook of strengthening, empowering patients to take part in their mending cycle effectively.

9. **Support Gatherings and Friend Organizations:**

Participating in help gatherings or associating with peers confronting comparable muscular difficulties gives an important road to consistent encouragement. Sharing encounters, trading survival methods, and building a feeling of local area add to worked on mental prosperity. Peer networks make a space where people feel comprehended and upheld, diminishing sensations of confinement.

The brain body association in help bunches includes perceiving the profound advantages of shared encounters and common help. Muscular consideration that energizes cooperation in help bunches recognizes the social and profound components of recuperating, encouraging a feeling of having a place and strength.

7.1 Recognizing the Emotional Toll of Orthopedic Issues

Perceiving the Close to home Cost of Muscular Issues: Exploring the Complicated Scene of Physical and Mental Prosperity

Muscular issues, including a range of conditions from breaks and joint issues to constant outer muscle problems, stretch out past the domain of actual inconvenience. The close to home cost of muscular issues is a huge and frequently disregarded part of the patient experience. This investigation digs into the complex exchange between actual agony, profound prosperity, and the more extensive effect on a person's psychological well-being, underscoring the significance of perceiving and tending to the close to home components of muscular difficulties.

1. **Actual Torment and Profound Pain:**

   The foundation of muscular issues lies in actual torment, a powerful variable that can prompt profound pain. The impression of torment, whether intense or ongoing, isn't simply a physiological reaction yet an intricate exchange of tangible and profound parts. People wrestling with muscular issues might encounter the unmistakable distress of torment as well as a scope of feelings, including dissatisfaction, tension, and even discouragement.

   The psyche body association in actual torment and close to home misery includes understanding what the view of agony means for a person's psychological state. Muscular consideration that perceives and addresses the close to home cost of actual agony adopts an all encompassing strategy, recognizing that easing profound pain is indispensable to the general prosperity of the patient.

2. **Disturbance to Day to day existence and Schedule:**

   Muscular issues frequently achieve a disturbance to day to day existence and schedules. Undertakings that were once commonplace and easy become difficulties, requiring changes and variations. The dissatisfaction and close to home effect of this interruption stretch out past the actual restrictions, affecting a singular's feeling of independence and freedom. Perceiving the profound cost of these disturbances is fundamental in giving sympathetic and exhaustive consideration.

   The psyche body association in the disturbance to day to day existence includes figuring out the profound meaning of routine and commonality. Muscular consideration that recognizes the profound effect of interruptions assists people with exploring the difficulties of adjusting to another ordinary, cultivating versatility and a positive mentality.

3. **Influence on Self-perception and Confidence:**

Muscular issues, particularly those including noticeable changes or the utilization of assistive gadgets, can significantly affect self-perception and confidence. People might encounter modified view of their bodies, prompting healthy identity cognizance or an insecurity. Tending to the profound elements of self-perception is significant in advancing a positive mental self portrait and keeping up with mental prosperity.

The psyche body association in the effect on self-perception includes perceiving the profound reactions to changes in actual appearance. Muscular consideration that integrates procedures to help positive self-perception contributes not exclusively to actual recuperation yet additionally to the profound versatility of people exploring muscular difficulties.

4. **Loss of Freedom and Independence:**

Muscular issues frequently involve a deficiency of freedom and independence, especially when people need help with day to day exercises or portability. The profound cost of depending on others for fundamental errands can prompt sensations of weakness, dissatisfaction, and a feeling of reliance. Perceiving and tending to the close to home effect of this misfortune is vital for thorough muscular consideration.

The psyche body association in the deficiency of freedom includes grasping the close to home meaning of independence. Muscular consideration that considers the close to home cost of reliance effectively pursues encouraging a feeling of organization and strengthening, adding to the psychological prosperity of people confronting muscular difficulties.

5. **Chronicity and Emotional well-being Difficulties:**

Ongoing muscular issues, portrayed by long haul or repeating conditions, present exceptional difficulties to psychological wellness. The industriousness of side effects, continuous medicines, and the vulnerability of long haul results can add to psychological well-being difficulties like uneasiness and discouragement. Tending to the close to home cost of chronicity is fundamental for supporting people in their excursion towards both physical and mental prosperity.

The brain body association in ongoing muscular issues includes perceiving the recurrent connection between actual side effects and emotional well-being difficulties. Muscular consideration that focuses on emotional well-being support for constant circumstances takes on a proactive methodology, recognizing that close to home prosperity is essential to the general administration of the condition.

6. **Relational Connections and Social Disconnection:**

   Muscular issues can impact relational connections, as people might confront difficulties in partaking in friendly exercises or keeping up with past degrees of commitment. The profound cost of social disconnection, whether purposeful or an outcome of actual limits, can add to sensations of forlornness and withdrawal. Perceiving the effect on relational connections is imperative for comprehensive muscular consideration.

   The psyche body association in relational connections includes figuring out the close to home meaning of social associations. Muscular consideration that tends to the potential for social seclusion effectively elevates systems to keep up with social commitment, cultivating profound prosperity and a feeling of connectedness.

7. **Dread and Nervousness Connected with Future Portability:**

   People confronting muscular issues, especially those including versatility concerns, may wrestle with dread and uneasiness in regards to their future portability. The vulnerability encompassing the capacity to recover full capability or worries about the potential for future restrictions can add to elevated feelings of anxiety. Recognizing and tending to these feelings of trepidation is fundamental for lightening nervousness and advancing mental flexibility.

   The psyche body association in dread and nervousness includes perceiving the close to home reactions to vulnerabilities about future versatility. Muscular consideration that coordinates techniques to address these feelings of trepidation cultivates a good mentality, enabling people to effectively take part in their recuperation process with certainty.

8. **Delayed Recovery and Tolerance:**

   Delayed recovery, a typical part of muscular consideration, can test a singular's understanding and strength. The close to home cost of exploring a lengthy recuperation interaction might prompt sensations of restlessness, disappointment, or even gloom.

   Perceiving the personal difficulties related with delayed restoration is pivotal for offering custom-made help and advancing mental prosperity.

   The psyche body association in delayed recovery includes figuring out the close to home elements of perseverance and persistence. Muscular consideration that tends to the profound cost of an extended recuperation process effectively elevates techniques to keep up with mental flexibility, cultivating an inspirational perspective regardless of the difficulties.

9. **Patient-Focused Correspondence and Compassion:**

Integral to perceiving and tending to the close to home cost of muscular issues shows restraint focused correspondence and compassion. Medical services suppliers who approach muscular consideration with sympathy and an emphasis on the person's close to home prosperity establish a steady climate. Open exchange that urges patients to communicate their apprehensions, concerns, and profound encounters is instrumental in giving customized and all encompassing consideration.

The brain body association in persistent focused correspondence includes figuring out the profound effect of sympathetic and mindful medical services cooperations. Muscular consideration that focuses on quiet focused correspondence effectively adds to the close to home prosperity of people confronting muscular difficulties.

7.2 Importance of Mental Health in Ortho Care

The Significance of Emotional wellness in Muscular Consideration: Cultivating All encompassing Prosperity through Exhaustive Help

Muscular consideration, customarily centered around diagnosing and treating actual illnesses influencing the outer muscle framework, is going through a change in outlook. Perceiving the significant effect of psychological well-being on the general prosperity of patients, the significance of tending to the mental elements of muscular consideration has come to the very front. This investigation dives into the complicated connection between psychological well-being and muscular consideration, underlining the requirement for a complete and coordinated approach that recognizes the indistinguishable association among physical and mental prosperity.

1. **The Interconnected Idea of Physical and Emotional well-being:**

   The human experience is innately entwined with the complicated interchange among physical and emotional well-being. Perceiving the interconnected idea of these aspects is especially vital with regards to muscular consideration. The outer muscle framework, involving bones, joints, muscles, and connective tissues, isn't disconnected from the impact of mental prosperity. Profound states, feelings of anxiety, and mental strength can altogether affect the direction of muscular circumstances and the viability of treatment plans.

   The psyche body association in muscular consideration includes understanding what psychological well-being means for actual wellbeing as well as the other way around. An extensive methodology that incorporates the two aspects perceives the cooperative connection among physical and mental prosperity, encouraging an all encompassing comprehension of patient consideration.

2. **Profound Reactions to Muscular Difficulties:**

   Muscular difficulties, whether coming about because of horrible wounds, ongoing circumstances, or careful mediations, bring out a scope of close to home reactions in patients. The experience of agony, disturbances to day to day existence, worries about versatility, and the vulnerability of recuperation can add to profound trouble. Tension, misery, disappointment, and dread are normal close to home reactions that can altogether influence the patient's general prosperity.

   The brain body association in profound reactions to muscular difficulties includes understanding how the mental parts of the patient's experience impact their actual recuperation. Recognizing and tending to these close to home reactions is crucial for giving patient-focused care that tends to both the substantial and elusive elements of muscular difficulties.

3. **Effect of Psychological well-being on Torment Discernment:**

   The impression of agony is unpredictably connected to psychological wellness. Close to home states, feelings of anxiety, and mental elements can tweak the power and resistance of agony. With regards to muscular consideration, where torment is a common side effect, understanding the impact of emotional wellness on torment insight becomes fundamental. Patients encountering profound trouble might see torment all the more intensely, making compelling torment the executives procedures a basic part of exhaustive muscular consideration.

   The brain body association in torment discernment includes perceiving that emotional well-being assumes a urgent part in forming the emotional experience of torment. Muscular consideration that considers the mental parts of agony insight works on the patient's solace as well as adds to a more certain and helpful outlook during the recuperation cycle.

4. **Psychosocial Elements and Treatment Results:**

   Psychosocial factors, enveloping angles like social help, survival techniques, and mental versatility, essentially impact treatment results in muscular consideration. Patients with vigorous social emotionally supportive networks and powerful survival methods frequently show better adherence to treatment plans, connect all the more effectively in restoration, and exhibit worked on generally speaking results. On the other hand, people confronting emotional well-being moves might encounter boundaries to compelling treatment, prompting subpar results.

   The brain body association in psychosocial variables and treatment results includes perceiving that emotional well-being is a determinant of the patient's commitment and obligation to the helpful cycle. Far reaching muscular consideration considers the psychosocial aspects, encouraging a climate that upgrades treatment viability and supports the patient's excursion toward recuperation.

5. **Viability of Restoration and Recuperation:**

   Restoration and recuperation in muscular consideration reach out past the actual recovery of outer muscle structures. The viability of recovery is intently attached to the patient's psychological prosperity. Inspiration, tirelessness, and a positive outlook assume crucial parts in accomplishing ideal restoration results. Patients with psychological well-being difficulties might confront obstacles in keeping up with consistency and excitement all through the restoration cycle, affecting the general progress of recuperation.

   The psyche body association in restoration and recuperation includes understanding that psychological wellness impacts the patient's capacity to effectively take part in and get benefits from recovery programs. Muscular consideration that focuses on the psychological prosperity of patients perceives the complementary connection between mental states and the adequacy of recovery endeavors.

6. **Forestalling and Tending to Emotional wellness Difficulties:**

   Proactive measures to forestall and address emotional well-being difficulties in muscular consideration are fundamental to cultivating comprehensive prosperity. Executing systems like routine emotional well-being screenings, early intercession for people in danger of mental pain, and giving admittance to psychological well-being assets add to a far reaching care model. Tending to psychological wellness challenges upgrades the patient's insight as well as emphatically impacts treatment results.

   The psyche body association in forestalling and tending to emotional wellness challenges includes perceiving the proactive job that muscular consideration can play in supporting mental prosperity. A patient-driven approach that focuses on psychological well-being adds to a more comprehensive and sympathetic medical care climate.

7. **Patient-Focused Correspondence and Sympathy:**

   Successful correspondence and sympathy are central components of patient-focused muscular consideration that thinks about emotional wellness. Medical services suppliers who participate in open and compassionate correspondence establish a strong climate where patients feel appreciated and comprehended. Recognizing the close to home parts of the patient's experience cultivates trust, energizes straightforwardness, and adds to a positive helpful coalition.

   The psyche body association in understanding focused correspondence includes perceiving that how data is conveyed can affect the patient's personal state and, subsequently, their general prosperity. Muscular consideration that puts accentuation on quiet focused correspondence recognizes the significance of cultivating a trusting and steady connection between medical services suppliers and patients.

8. **Incorporating Psychological well-being Backing into Muscular Practices:**

   The mix of emotional well-being support into muscular practices is a groundbreaking step towards thorough patient consideration. This includes cooperation with emotional wellness experts, integrating psychological well-being appraisals into routine muscular assessments, and giving admittance to advising or psychotherapy when required. Embracing a multidisciplinary approach guarantees that the patient gets all encompassing consideration that tends to both physical and mental parts of their prosperity.

   The psyche body association in coordinating psychological wellness support includes perceiving that emotional well-being is certainly not a different substance however a fundamental piece of the patient's general wellbeing. Muscular consideration that consistently incorporates psychological well-being support mirrors a promise to giving thorough and patient-driven administrations.

9. **Instructive Drives for Patients and Parental figures:**

Instructive drives that engage patients and guardians with information about the interconnected idea of physical and psychological well-being add to proactive muscular consideration. Giving data about the likely close to home reactions to muscular difficulties, systems for adapting to emotional wellness difficulties, and assets for looking for help upgrades the patient's capacity to explore their muscular excursion with versatility and informed direction.

The brain body association in instructive drives includes perceiving the job of information in molding the's comprehension patient might interpret their well-being. Muscular consideration that focuses on understanding training recognizes the strengthening that accompanies informed direction and dynamic cooperation in the recuperating system.

7.3 Collaborative Approaches in Treatment

Cooperative Methodologies in Muscular Treatment: Exploring the Intricacies with a Brought together Front

Muscular therapy, portrayed by its diverse nature, requests a cooperative methodology that reaches out past the bounds of a solitary clinical strength. This investigation dives into the meaning of cooperative methodologies in muscular consideration, featuring the interconnectedness of different medical services trains, the advantages of a multidisciplinary group, and the groundbreaking effect on understanding results.

1. **The Interconnected Idea of Muscular Circumstances:**

   Muscular circumstances frequently present an embroidery of intricacies, entwining different features of outer muscle wellbeing. Perceiving the interconnected idea of these circumstances, where a brokenness in one perspective can resound across the whole framework, highlights the requirement for cooperative methodologies. Whether tending to intense wounds, constant problems, or post-careful recovery, understanding the all encompassing ramifications of muscular issues establishes the groundwork for a brought together and complete therapy technique.

   The psyche body association in muscular circumstances includes recognizing that actual afflictions can significantly affect mental prosperity as well as the other way around. A cooperative methodology lines up with the comprehensive comprehension that the complexities of muscular consideration reach out past the limits of a solitary clinical strength, requiring coordinated effort among different medical services experts.

2. **The Multidisciplinary Group in Muscular Consideration:**

   A foundation of cooperative methodologies in muscular consideration is the development of a multidisciplinary group. Including muscular specialists, actual advisors, word related advisors, torment subject matter experts, clinicians, nutritionists, and other united medical care experts, this group joins different mastery to address the multi-layered necessities of the patient. Every part contributes exceptional experiences and mediations, making an exhaustive consideration plan custom fitted to the singular's particular muscular difficulties.

The brain body association in a multidisciplinary group includes perceiving that the patient's actual wellbeing is unpredictably connected to their psychological and profound prosperity. A cooperative methodology guarantees that the all encompassing components of muscular consideration are tended to, cultivating a more nuanced comprehension of the patient's general wellbeing.

3. **Muscular Specialists: Heads of the Cooperative Group:**
Muscular specialists act as pioneers inside the cooperative group, guiding the course of conclusion, treatment arranging, and careful mediations. Their mastery in outer muscle wellbeing is crucial in directing the general course of muscular consideration. Cooperative methodologies stress the dynamic contribution of muscular specialists in interdisciplinary conversations, guaranteeing that their bits of knowledge advise the more extensive range regarding care gave to the patient.

The psyche body association with muscular specialists in charge includes perceiving the focal job they play in tending to both the physical and close to home parts of muscular circumstances. Cooperative methodologies enable muscular specialists to lead a group that on the whole tends to the intricacies intrinsic in outer muscle wellbeing.

4. **Actual Specialists: Coordinating Restoration and Utilitarian Recuperation:**
Actual specialists assume a vital part in the cooperative way to deal with muscular consideration, especially in the domain of restoration and practical recuperation. Their ability in planning custom fitted activity regimens, further developing scope of movement, and addressing outer muscle irregular characteristics contributes essentially to the patient's excursion towards ideal recuperation. Cooperative methodologies guarantee that actual specialists work couple with other medical care experts to adjust recovery objectives to more extensive therapy goals.

The psyche body association in exercise based recuperation includes perceiving that the actual restoration process is unpredictably connected to the patient's psychological prosperity. Cooperative methodologies permit actual specialists to effectively add to an all encompassing consideration plan, advancing both physical and profound flexibility in patients.

5. **Word related Advisors: Upgrading Everyday Usefulness:**
Cooperative methodologies in muscular consideration reach out to the contribution of word related specialists, who center around improving a singular's

capacity to take part in everyday exercises. Tending to actual impediments as well as considering the more extensive effect on way of life and freedom, word related specialists add to a more exhaustive and patient-driven care plan. Cooperation guarantees that the objectives set by word related specialists line up with the general treatment goals of the multidisciplinary group.

The brain body association in word related treatment includes figuring out the close to home meaning of everyday exercises and autonomy. Cooperative methodologies permit word related specialists to work cooperatively with different experts, adding to a more nuanced comprehension of the patient's practical requirements and profound prosperity.

6. **Torment Subject matter experts: Overseeing Complex Agony Conditions:**
Persistent agony frequently goes with muscular circumstances, requiring particular mediations from torment subject matter experts. Cooperative methodologies consolidate the mastery of torment the executives experts who center around a complex comprehension of torment. By tending to the actual cause of torment as well as the close to home and mental parts, torment experts add to a more all encompassing way to deal with muscular consideration.

The brain body association in torment the board includes perceiving that successful aggravation control isn't exclusively about tending to the actual sensations yet in addition includes contemplations of the patient's close to home prosperity. Cooperative methodologies engage torment experts to work cooperatively with the more extensive group, guaranteeing that aggravation the board lines up with the general objectives of thorough muscular consideration.

7. **Analysts: Tending to Emotional well-being in Muscular Consideration:**
Cooperative methodologies recognize the essential job of analysts in tending to the emotional well-being parts of muscular consideration.

Close to home reactions to muscular difficulties, like uneasiness, misery, or change hardships, are appropriately tended to by clinicians. Teaming up with other medical services experts guarantees that mental intercessions are flawlessly coordinated into the more extensive therapy plan, cultivating a comprehensive way to deal with patient consideration.

The brain body association in mental mediations includes perceiving that psychological wellness is an essential determinant of in general prosperity. Cooperative methodologies empower clinicians to contribute their mastery to the multidisciplinary group, guaranteeing that the close to home elements of muscular consideration are given due thought.

8. **Nutritionists: Advancing Recuperating Through Diet:**
Nourishment assumes a urgent part in the recuperating system, particularly in muscular consideration where sufficient supplements support tissue fix and recuperation. Cooperative methodologies include the consideration of nutritionists who contribute their aptitude in improving dietary intends to upgrade

the recuperating system. By adjusting dietary procedures to the particular requirements of muscular patients, cooperative consideration tends to both the physical and nourishing parts of recuperation.

The psyche body association in nourishment includes perceiving that dietary decisions influence actual wellbeing as well as profound prosperity. Cooperative methodologies guarantee that nutritionists work pair with other medical services experts, adding to a far reaching care plan that advances comprehensive mending.

9. **Patient-Focused Correspondence and Shared Independent direction:**
Cooperative methodologies focus on understanding focused correspondence and shared decision-production as crucial standards. Perceiving the significance of including patients in choices about their consideration, cooperative groups take part in open exchange that thinks about the patient's inclinations, values, and objectives. This approach cultivates a feeling of strengthening, imparting trust in patients as dynamic members in their muscular excursion.

The psyche body association in understanding focused correspondence includes perceiving that how data is conveyed can affect the patient's actual prosperity as well as their close to home state. Cooperative methodologies guarantee that correspondence lines up with the standards of shared direction, advancing a more comprehensive and patient-driven care model.

10. **Coherence of Care and Consistent Advances:**

Cooperative methodologies in muscular consideration focus on progression of care and consistent changes between various periods of treatment. From careful intercessions to restoration and continuous administration, a strong arrangement guarantees that the patient encounters a smooth change between different medical services experts. This congruity encourages a feeling of trust and certainty, adding to the general viability of muscular consideration.

The brain body association in progression of care includes perceiving that disturbances in the medical services excursion can affect actual results as well as profound prosperity. Cooperative methodologies focus on a consistent continuum of care, guaranteeing that the patient encounters a bound together and durable excursion towards recuperation.

7.4 Therapeutic Techniques for Coping

Restorative Procedures for Adapting to Muscular Difficulties: Supporting Flexibility and Prosperity

Muscular difficulties, set apart by actual inconvenience and profound pressure, require a comprehensive methodology that goes past customary clinical mediations. This investigation dives into remedial methods intended to assist people with adapting to the intricacies of muscular circumstances. From mental procedures to actual intercessions, these survival techniques mean to cultivate versatility, improve prosperity, and engage people on their excursion towards recuperation.

1. **Care and Unwinding Methods:**

   Care, established in the act of being available in the ongoing second without judgment, offers an amazing asset for adapting to muscular difficulties. People confronting outer muscle uneasiness can profit from care and unwinding strategies, which incorporate practices like profound breathing, moderate muscle unwinding, and directed symbolism. These methods give a reprieve from actual inconvenience as well as add to close to home prosperity by lessening pressure and advancing a feeling of quiet.

   The brain body association in care includes perceiving that psychological prosperity is unpredictably connected to actual sensations. Integrating care into survival techniques empowers people to explore muscular difficulties with more noteworthy close to home strength and an elevated feeling of mindfulness.

2. **Mental Conduct Treatment (CBT):**

   Mental Conduct Treatment (CBT) is a remedial methodology that objectives the interaction between contemplations, sentiments, and ways of behaving. With regards to muscular difficulties, CBT can be instrumental in tending to negative idea designs, overseeing torment related pain, and encouraging versatile survival techniques. By investigating the mental and close to home elements of muscular circumstances, people can reexamine their viewpoints, construct versatility, and foster powerful techniques for overseeing both physical and profound parts of their wellbeing.

   The brain body association in CBT includes understanding how mental cycles impact profound reactions and, thus, actual prosperity. Coordinating CBT into adapting methods enables people to effectively shape their psychological and close to home scene, decidedly affecting their general involvement in muscular difficulties.

3. **Biofeedback and Neurofeedback:**

   Biofeedback and neurofeedback are restorative procedures that use constant checking of physiological reactions to improve self-guideline. With regards to muscular difficulties, these strategies can be applied to oversee pressure, tension, and agony. By giving people visual or hear-able criticism on physiological boundaries, for example, pulse, muscle strain, or brainwave movement, biofeedback and neurofeedback enable people to oversee their physiological reactions, adding to a feeling of organization in adapting to muscular circumstances.

   The brain body association in biofeedback and neurofeedback includes perceiving the equal connection between physiological states and profound encounters. These procedures offer an unmistakable means for people to regulate their physiological reactions, advancing a feeling of control and prosperity in the midst of muscular difficulties.

4. **Workmanship and Expressive Treatments:**
Craftsmanship and expressive treatments give an imaginative outlet to people wrestling with muscular difficulties. Whether through visual expressions, music, dance, or composing, expressive treatments offer a method for self-articulation and profound delivery. Taking part in imaginative exercises can act as an interruption from actual distress, cultivate a feeling of achievement, and give people a medium to investigate and deal with their feelings connected with muscular circumstances.

The psyche body association in craftsmanship and expressive treatments includes perceiving the helpful worth of imaginative articulation in advancing close to home prosperity. Integrating these procedures into survival methods urges people to take advantage of their innovative potential, adding to a more comprehensive way to deal with overseeing muscular difficulties.

5. **Yoga and Development Treatments:**
Yoga and development treatments offer an all encompassing way to deal with adapting to muscular difficulties by joining active work with care and breath mindfulness. These practices stress delicate developments, extending, and reinforcing practices custom-made to oblige people with outer muscle issues. Yoga, specifically, has been displayed to decrease torment, further develop adaptability, and upgrade in general prosperity. The incorporation of careful development can decidedly affect both the physical and close to home elements of muscular circumstances.

The brain body association in yoga and development treatments includes perceiving how actual developments and breath mindfulness impact profound states. Integrating these practices into ways of dealing with stress tends to actual inconvenience as well as adds to a feeling of encapsulation and equilibrium in the midst of muscular difficulties.

6. **Support Gatherings and Companion Connection:**
Social help is a critical part of adapting to muscular difficulties. Participating in help gatherings or interfacing with peers confronting comparative issues gives a feeling of kinship, understanding, and shared encounters. Through these co-operations, people can acquire bits of knowledge into survival techniques, share ways of dealing with especially difficult times that have worked for them, and get consistent reassurance, encouraging a feeling of having a place and strength.

The brain body association in help bunches includes perceiving the effect of social associations on close to home prosperity. Taking part in help bunches upgrades the profound element of adapting, offering people a stage to share their difficulties, praise victories, and draw strength from the aggregate encounters of others confronting muscular circumstances.

7. **Torment The board Strategies:**

Torment the board strategies envelop a scope of intercessions pointed toward easing actual inconvenience related with muscular difficulties. These may incorporate pharmacological methodologies, non-intrusive treatments, and elective modalities like needle therapy or back rub. Powerful agony the board not just addresses the actual part of muscular circumstances yet additionally adds to profound prosperity by diminishing the effect of agony on day to day existence and in general personal satisfaction.

The brain body association in torment the executives includes perceiving that compelling aggravation control emphatically impacts close to home states. Incorporating torment the executives methods into ways of dealing with especially difficult times guarantees a more thorough methodology, tending to both the physical and close to home elements of muscular difficulties.

8. **Journaling and Reflection:**

Journaling and intelligent practices furnish people with a way to investigate and handle their feelings connected with muscular difficulties. Expounding on encounters, considerations, and sentiments considers self-reflection, close to home articulation, and the distinguishing proof of examples in adapting. Journaling can act as a remedial outlet, supporting people in acquiring lucidity, cultivating mindfulness, and advancing close to home prosperity.

The brain body association in journaling includes perceiving the job of intelligent practices in molding close to home encounters. Consolidating journaling into adapting strategies urges people to take part in contemplation, adding to a more nuanced comprehension of their close to home reactions to muscular difficulties.

9. **Mind-Body Mediations:**

Mind-body mediations, like reflection and yoga, accentuate the association among mental and actual prosperity. These practices incorporate breath control, reflection, and delicate developments to advance unwinding, diminish pressure, and improve by and large flexibility.

Mind-body intercessions offer people an all encompassing way to deal with adapting to muscular difficulties, tending to both the actual uneasiness and close to home parts of their experience.

The brain body association as a top priority body mediations includes perceiving how purposeful practices impact both mental and actual states. Integrating these intercessions into survival methods engages people to develop a careful and typified way to deal with exploring muscular difficulties.

Chapter 8

Peer Support and Teen Ortho Wellness

Peer Backing and Adolescent Muscular Health: Exploring Pre-adulthood Together

Youthfulness is an extraordinary stage set apart by actual changes, inner disturbances, and the mission for personality. When compounded with muscular difficulties, young people frequently face one of a kind obstacles that stretch out past the actual domain. Peer support arises as an imperative part in exploring these intricacies, encouraging strength, sympathy, and a feeling of local area among teenagers wrestling with muscular circumstances.

1. **The Young adult Muscular Scene:**

   Puberty is a basic period portrayed by quick actual development, hormonal vacillations, and the improvement of self-character. Muscular difficulties during this time can appear in different structures, from sports-related wounds to outer muscle conditions like scoliosis. The convergence of muscular issues and the wild scene of immaturity makes an extraordinary arrangement of difficulties that reach out past the clinical space.

   The brain body association in juvenile muscular health includes perceiving the perplexing exchange between actual wellbeing and close to home prosperity. Peer support turns into an extension that tends to the actual parts of muscular difficulties as well as the profound aspects, offering a mutual perspective of the excursion youngsters face.

2. **The Meaning of Companion Backing:**

   Peer support holds gigantic importance in the domain of juvenile muscular health. Young people frequently go to their friends for approval, understanding, and shared encounters. With regards to muscular difficulties, peers become a wellspring of compassion, support, and a feeling of business as usual, relieving the sensations of confinement that can go with actual medical problems.

The brain body association in peer support includes perceiving the job of profound prosperity in the in general muscular experience. At the point when young people interface with peers confronting comparative difficulties, they find useful guidance as well as a common close to home language that adds to their comprehensive prosperity.

3. **Building a Feeling of Local area:**

   Peer support makes a feeling of local area among young people exploring muscular difficulties. The foundation of this local area is essential in scattering sensations of estrangement and cultivating a space where people can straightforwardly examine their encounters, share survival methods, and celebrate triumphs. This feeling of having a place adds to close to home strength and an uplifting perspective on the excursion of muscular wellbeing.

   The psyche body association in building a feeling of local area includes perceiving that profound prosperity is sustained through a steady friendly climate. Peer support drives, whether face to face or on the web, make stages for youngsters to interface, offer, and construct a local area that gets it and approves their muscular encounters.

4. **Compassion and Understanding:**

   Peer support develops sympathy and understanding among youngsters confronting muscular difficulties. Peers who share comparative encounters can connect with the close to home ups and downs, giving a degree of understanding that might be trying to achieve from those without comparable encounters. This common perspective cultivates a caring climate where teens feel seen, heard, and approved.

   The psyche body association in compassion and understanding includes perceiving that basic reassurance is entwined with actual prosperity. The sympathetic association between peers offers comfort as well as a substantial effect on the close to home flexibility expected to explore the intricacies of muscular difficulties during youth.

5. **Exploring Social Elements:**

   Youthfulness is when social elements assume an essential part in molding confidence and social character. Muscular difficulties can impact how young people see themselves in friendly settings, possibly prompting reluctance or disconnection. Peer support goes about as an impetus for exploring these social elements, giving a stage to teens to examine the difficulties they face and plan ways of connecting with certainty in friendly exercises.

   The psyche body association in exploring social elements includes perceiving the corresponding connection between close to home prosperity and social cooperations. Peer support outfits teens with the devices to explore social difficulties, cultivating a positive mentality that adds to their generally speaking muscular health.

6. **Shared Survival techniques:**

Peer support fills in as a storehouse of shared survival techniques. Teens confronting muscular difficulties frequently experience special circumstances that require imaginative arrangements. Peers who have explored comparative circumstances can offer functional counsel, methods for dealing with especially difficult times, and procedures for overseeing both the physical and close to home parts of muscular circumstances.

The psyche body association in shared methods for dealing with stress includes perceiving that profound prosperity is supported when people approach a toolbox of powerful survival strategies. Peer support turns into a significant asset in such manner, enabling young people with bits of knowledge and procedures that add to their versatility notwithstanding muscular difficulties.

7. **Advancing Dynamic Commitment:**

Peer support advances dynamic commitment among youngsters in their muscular health venture. Rather than latently persevering through their circumstances, teens effectively take part in conversations, share encounters, and add to the aggregate information inside the companion support local area. This dynamic commitment cultivates a feeling of organization and strengthening, decidedly impacting both their close to home and actual prosperity.

The brain body association in advancing dynamic commitment includes perceiving that a proactive way to deal with muscular health adds to a positive close to home state. Peer support urges teens to play a functioning job in their wellbeing, making a feeling of pride and strengthening in dealing with their muscular circumstances.

8. **Peer Tutoring and Job Demonstrating:**

Peer support presents the idea of friend coaching, where people who have effectively explored muscular difficulties become good examples for those right now confronting comparable issues.

The trading of encounters, experiences, and examples of overcoming adversity makes a positive story that motivates trust, flexibility, and a feeling of probability among young people managing muscular circumstances.

The psyche body association in peer tutoring includes perceiving the impact of positive good examples on profound prosperity. Peer tutors offer reasonable exhortation as well as everyday encouragement, adding to the generally speaking mental versatility of young people wrestling with muscular difficulties.

9. **Working with Open Correspondence:**

Peer support works with open correspondence about muscular difficulties, separating the hindrances of shame and quiet. Youngsters can communicate their interests, share their victories, and examine the close to home parts of their excursion unafraid of judgment. This open correspondence advances close to home prosperity by establishing a climate where youngsters feel happy with talking about the effect of muscular circumstances on their lives.

The brain body association in open correspondence includes perceiving that profound prosperity flourishes in a climate of open discourse. Peer support drives make spaces where teens can uninhibitedly offer their viewpoints and sentiments, cultivating a feeling of close to home delivery and association.

8.1 Building a Supportive Community

Building a Steady People group for Muscular Health: Encouraging Associations and Strength

Muscular difficulties, whether emerging from wounds or constant circumstances, can fundamentally affect a person's physical and close to home prosperity. The formation of a strong local area is instrumental in exploring these difficulties, offering an organization of figuring out, compassion, and shared encounters. This investigation dives into the significance of building a strong local area for muscular wellbeing, underscoring the interconnected idea of physical and close to home wellbeing.

1. **The All encompassing Effect of Muscular Difficulties:**

   Muscular difficulties envelop a range of conditions that influence the outer muscle framework, including bones, joints, tendons, muscles, and ligaments. Whether it's recuperating from a games injury, overseeing ongoing circumstances like joint pain, or adapting to post-careful recovery, the effect reaches out past actual uneasiness. Close to home prosperity becomes entwined with the experience, featuring the requirement for an extensive and steady way to deal with muscular wellbeing.

   The brain body association in muscular difficulties includes perceiving what actual wellbeing means for profound states as well as the other way around. Building a steady local area recognizes this interconnectedness, establishing a climate that tends to the two elements of prosperity.

2. **Mutual perspective and Sympathy:**

   A strong local area for muscular wellbeing gives a stage to common perspective and compassion. People inside the local area have firsthand involvement in the difficulties of muscular circumstances, making a space where shared understanding flourishes. The sympathy that rises up out of shared encounters cultivates a feeling of association, easing the sensations of disconnection that people with muscular difficulties might confront.

   The psyche body association in common perspective includes perceiving that close to home prosperity is enhanced when people feel seen and grasped in their actual battles. Building a steady local area develops a climate where sympathy prospers, adding to a positive profound state.

3. **Online Stages and Companion Associations:**

   In the computerized age, online stages assume a significant part in building strong networks for muscular health. Gatherings, online entertainment gatherings, and virtual networks give roads to people to interface with peers confronting comparable difficulties. These stages separate geological boundaries, empowering a different scope of people to share bits of knowledge, trade exhortation, and proposition daily reassurance.

The brain body association in web-based stages includes perceiving the mental effect of virtual associations. Building a strong local area online gives functional data as well as makes a feeling of having a place and shared personality, emphatically impacting profound prosperity.

4. **Support Gatherings and Instructive Assets:**
   Support gatherings, both on the web and face to face, act as essential parts of a steady local area for muscular wellbeing. These gatherings offer an organized climate for people to share encounters, examine survival techniques, and access instructive assets. Notwithstanding basic reassurance, support bunches give significant data about overseeing muscular circumstances, exploring medicines, and advancing generally speaking prosperity.

   The brain body association in help bunches includes perceiving that information and basic reassurance are entwined. Admittance to instructive assets enables people to come to informed conclusions about their actual wellbeing, adding to a feeling of control and organization in their muscular health venture.

5. **Local area Based Occasions and Exercises:**
   Building a strong local area stretches out past virtual collaborations to incorporate local area based occasions and exercises. Whether it's coordinated strolls, studios, or health withdraws, these social affairs set out open doors for people to associate face to face, share stories, and participate in exercises that advance physical and profound prosperity. The feeling of brotherhood created in such settings adds to a steady organization that rises above the computerized domain. The psyche body association in local area based occasions includes perceiving the effect of social cooperations on profound prosperity. Participating in exercises with others cultivates a feeling of local area, happiness, and shared achievement, decidedly impacting the profound condition of people with muscular difficulties.

6. **Promotion and Strengthening Drives:**
   Building a strong local area includes support and strengthening drives that intensify the voices of people with muscular difficulties. By pushing for comprehensive strategies, openness, and mindfulness, the local area turns into a power for change that emphatically impacts both the physical and profound parts of muscular wellbeing. Strengthening drives center around encouraging flexibility, self-backing, and a deep satisfaction in one's excursion.

   The brain body association in promotion includes perceiving that social help adds to a positive profound state. At the point when people feel enabled and upheld by a local area that comprehends their difficulties, the close to home effect of muscular circumstances is relieved, adding to generally speaking prosperity.

7. **Patient-Focused Medical services Approach:**

A steady local area assumes an essential part in advancing a patient-focused way to deal with medical care. People inside the local area share bits of knowledge about their encounters with medical care suppliers, therapies, and restoration systems. This aggregate information enables people to partake in their medical services choices, cultivating a feeling of organization with medical care experts effectively.

The psyche body association in a patient-focused approach includes perceiving the impact of profound prosperity on treatment results. A strong local area adds to a positive outlook, upgrading the singular's capacity to participate in their medical services venture with strength and good faith.

8. **Developing Flexibility through Shared Stories:**

Shared stories inside a strong local area act as integral assets for developing flexibility. People sharing their accounts of beating difficulties, embracing energy, and finding strength become signals of motivation for other people.

These accounts add to an aggregate story of strength that supports that muscular difficulties don't characterize people however become vital pieces of their excursions.

The brain body association in shared stories includes perceiving the mental effect of accounts on close to home prosperity. Building a strong local area empowers the development of strength through shared stories, cultivating an inspirational perspective and versatile ways of dealing with stress.

9. **All encompassing Wellbeing Projects:**

All encompassing wellbeing programs inside a strong local area perceive the interconnected idea of physical and profound wellbeing. These projects might incorporate a mix of proactive tasks, care rehearses, and instructive meetings. By tending to the two elements of prosperity, all encompassing wellbeing programs add to a more complete methodology that upgrades the general personal satisfaction for people with muscular difficulties.

The psyche body association in all encompassing health programs includes perceiving that physical and close to home prosperity are reciprocal parts of by and large wellbeing. Building a strong local area that coordinates all encompassing health programs makes a space where people can flourish in the two components of their prosperity.

8.2 The Role of Peers in Ortho Recovery

The Significant Job of Friends in Muscular Recuperation: A Steady Organization for Mending and Strength

Muscular recuperation is a complex excursion that stretches out past actual restoration, incorporating close to home versatility and mental prosperity. In this comprehensive way to deal with recuperating, the job of friends becomes essential. The interconnectedness of physical and close to home aspects requires a steady organization that figures out the difficulties of muscular recuperation. This investigation digs into the significant job of friends in muscular recuperation, underscoring the meaning of compassion, shared encounters, and aggregate strength.

1. **Understanding the Muscular Recuperation Scene:**
   Muscular recuperation includes the reclamation of outer muscle wellbeing after wounds, medical procedures, or constant circumstances. This excursion frequently incorporates non-intrusive treatment, restoration works out, and a continuous re-visitation of day to day exercises. Notwithstanding, the close to home parts of muscular recuperation, like dissatisfaction, uneasiness, and the mental effect of actual constraints, are similarly critical. Peers, who share comparative encounters, become priceless colleagues on this complicated way to recuperation.

   The brain body association in muscular recuperation includes perceiving that profound prosperity is entwined with actual mending. Peers add to an extensive methodology by tending to the actual difficulties as well as the close to home parts of the recuperation cycle.

2. **Compassion and Shared Encounters:**
   Peers in muscular recuperation give a one of a kind wellspring of sympathy conceived out of shared encounters. Individual people who have confronted comparable wounds, medical procedures, or restoration challenges intrinsically comprehend the physical and profound rollercoaster of recuperation. This common perspective makes a groundwork of sympathy, offering a degree of help that goes past what can be given by the individuals who haven't gone through a comparative excursion.

   The psyche body association in compassion includes perceiving that consistent encouragement is a significant part of the recuperation cycle. Peers add to the profound prosperity of people by giving compassion established in their common encounters, cultivating a feeling of kinship and understanding.

3. **Inspiration and Motivation:**
   Peers assume a spurring and motivational part in muscular recuperation. Seeing other people who have effectively explored comparative difficulties and accomplished their recuperation objectives fills in as a strong wellspring of motivation. The examples of overcoming adversity inside the friend bunch become encouraging signs, imparting certainty and inspiration in people who might be wrestling with questions or mishaps in their own recuperation process.

   The brain body association in inspiration includes perceiving that a positive outlook adds to actual prosperity. Peers rouse people to develop strength, drive forward through difficulties, and keep a proactive way to deal with their recuperation, decidedly impacting both their psychological and actual states.

4. **Down to earth Exhortation and Survival methods:**

Peers offer down to earth exhortation and survival techniques in light of their firsthand encounters with muscular recuperation. From exploring everyday exercises to overseeing torment, peers share bits of knowledge into what has worked for them, giving important data that goes past clinical proposals. This trade of reasonable counsel turns into a cooperative exertion where people can draw from the aggregate insight of the individuals who have strolled a comparative way.

The brain body association in commonsense counsel includes perceiving that information about powerful survival methods adds to close to home flexibility. Peers act as guides in the improvement of versatile methods for dealing with hardship or stress, tending to the actual difficulties as well as the profound complexities of muscular recuperation.

5. **Making a Steady Biological system:**

Peers add to the production of a steady environment inside muscular recuperation networks. Whether in recovery habitats, support gatherings, or online stages, the aggregate comprehension among peers encourages a feeling of local area.

This biological system gives a place of refuge to people to share weaknesses, express worries, and celebrate achievements, establishing a climate where the close to home elements of recuperation are recognized and tended to.

The brain body association in a strong biological system includes perceiving that close to home prosperity flourishes locally where people feel appreciated and upheld. Peers add to the development of this steady climate, improving the general insight of muscular recuperation.

6. **Diminishing Sensations of Separation:**

Muscular recuperation can be detaching, particularly when people feel that their encounters are extraordinary or misconstrued. Peers ease sensations of confinement by offering a local area where people acknowledge they are in good company in their difficulties. Interfacing with other people who are on a comparative excursion standardizes the profound promising and less promising times of recuperation, giving a feeling of having a place that mitigates the disconnecting effect of muscular circumstances.

The psyche body association in lessening confinement includes perceiving that social associations add to close to home prosperity. Peers become friends in the recuperation venture, cultivating a feeling of association that emphatically impacts both the profound and actual parts of mending.

7. **Profound Flexibility and Shared Wins:**

The profound versatility developed inside peer bunches turns into a foundation of muscular recuperation. Shared wins, regardless of how little, are commended by and large, building up a positive story of progress and flexibility. Peers become observers to one another's triumphs, adding to a common pride that elevates the profound prosperity of the whole local area.

The psyche body association in profound flexibility includes perceiving that a positive close to home state improves actual prosperity. Peers assume a vital part in establishing a climate where people can recognize and commend their triumphs, adding to a general feeling of close to home prosperity.

8. **Adapting to Mishaps and Difficulties:**

Muscular recuperation is frequently set apart by mishaps and difficulties. Peers offer an imperative help framework during these troublesome times, offering figuring out, consolation, and a common point of view on conquering hindrances. Adapting to mishaps turns into an aggregate exertion where people draw strength from the flexibility of their companions, encouraging a feeling of trust and assurance.

The brain body association in adapting to mishaps includes perceiving that consistent encouragement is fundamental during testing periods of recuperation. Peers add to the close to home prosperity of people by offering comfort, support, and pragmatic counsel to explore difficulties and arise more grounded on the opposite side.

9. **Building Enduring Associations:**

Peer connections fashioned during muscular recuperation frequently stretch out past the bounds of recovery focuses or online gatherings. The enduring associations worked with peers become a demonstration of the getting through effect of shared encounters. These associations, established in sympathy and a common excursion, keep on offering profound help even after the conventional phases of recuperation have finished up.

The psyche body association in enduring associations includes perceiving that social bonds add to long haul profound prosperity. Peers become a fundamental piece of one another's lives, making an organization of help that rises above the quick difficulties of muscular recuperation.

8.3 Reducing Stigma and Fostering Empathy

Diminishing Shame and Encouraging Compassion in Muscular Wellbeing: A Call for Inclusivity and Understanding

Muscular wellbeing challenges frequently worry about actual concerns as well as the heaviness of cultural discernments and misinterpretations. Shame encompassing outer muscle conditions can fuel the profound cost for people exploring muscular excursions. This investigation dives into the significance of diminishing disgrace and encouraging sympathy in muscular wellbeing, underscoring the interconnected idea of physical and profound prosperity and upholding for a more comprehensive and grasping society.

1. **The Shame Encompassing Muscular Wellbeing:**
   Outer muscle conditions, going from ongoing issues like joint pain to intense wounds and medical procedures, are much of the time joined by cultural marks of shame. Dissimilar to some other ailments, muscular difficulties can be more apparent, prompting likely judgment or misinterpretations about people confronting these issues. Shame might appear in different structures, for example, suspicions around one's capacities, hesitance to take part in open discussions about muscular wellbeing, or even the impression of muscular circumstances as simply physical without recognizing the profound effect.

   The psyche body association in muscular wellbeing disgrace includes perceiving that cultural perspectives toward actual wellbeing can essentially impact profound prosperity. Decreasing shame becomes vital for establishing a more merciful climate as well as for decidedly influencing the psychological and close to home parts of muscular wellbeing.

2. **The Close to home Cost of Disgrace:**
   Disgrace encompassing muscular wellbeing can add to a close to home cost for people previously wrestling with actual difficulties. Sensations of disgrace, hesitance, or deficiency might emerge because of cultural perspectives or assumptions. This close to home weight can influence psychological wellness, possibly prompting tension, melancholy, or a reduced identity worth.

   The psyche body association in the close to home cost of shame includes perceiving that pessimistic cultural discernments can substantially affect profound prosperity. Encouraging sympathy and lessening shame turns into a method for lightening this close to home weight, making a space where people can explore muscular wellbeing challenges with nobility and versatility.

3. **Tending to Misinterpretations About Capacities:**
   Disgrace frequently comes from misinterpretations about the capacities of people confronting muscular difficulties. Presumptions about constraints or capacities in view of noticeable circumstances can add to an absence of understanding. Testing these misguided judgments and feature the different scope of capacities and qualities that people with muscular circumstances possess is urgent.

   The psyche body association in tending to confusions includes perceiving that the view of one's capacities can affect close to home prosperity. By encouraging sympathy and dissipating confusions, society can add to a more certain and enabling climate for people exploring muscular wellbeing challenges.

4. **Advancing Open Exchange:**
   Encouraging sympathy in muscular wellbeing requires advancing transparent

exchange. Empowering discussions about outer muscle conditions, recuperation ventures, and the close to home parts of muscular wellbeing helps end down the walls of quiet and mystery. At the point when people feel happy with sharing their encounters, it adds to a seriously understanding and strong cultural environment.

The brain body association in advancing open exchange includes perceiving that correspondence is fundamental to close to home prosperity. By encouraging open discussions, society can effectively add to decreasing disgrace and establishing a climate where people with muscular circumstances feel appreciated and comprehended.

5. **Instructing People in general:**

Training assumes a key part in lessening disgrace encompassing muscular wellbeing. Public mindfulness crusades, instructive drives, and local area outreach endeavors can give exact data about different outer muscle conditions, the difficulties people might confront, and the flexibility showed all through their excursions. Expanded information cultivates sympathy, dissipates fantasies, and adds to a more educated and sympathetic culture.

The psyche body association in teaching people in general includes perceiving that information is a useful asset for molding mentalities. By giving precise data about muscular wellbeing, society can effectively add to lessening disgrace and advancing a culture of sympathy and understanding.

6. **Making Comprehensive Spaces:**

Building comprehensive spaces is fundamental for encouraging sympathy in muscular wellbeing. Public spots, work environments, and sporting facilities ought to be planned in light of availability, guaranteeing that people with muscular difficulties can explore these spaces serenely. Establishing a climate that considers the different necessities of people encourages a feeling of inclusivity and decreases the potential for trashing.

The psyche body association in making comprehensive spaces includes perceiving that actual conditions can affect close to home prosperity. At the point when spaces are planned in view of inclusivity, people with muscular circumstances can explore their environmental elements with a feeling of pride and having a place.

7. **Advancing Sympathy in Medical care:**

Sympathy inside the medical care framework is essential for decreasing shame and encouraging comprehension. Medical services experts assume a urgent part in forming discernments and perspectives toward muscular wellbeing. By exhibiting sympathy, effectively paying attention to patients' encounters, and taking into account the profound components of muscular difficulties, medical services suppliers add to a more humane and strong medical services climate.

The psyche body association in advancing sympathy in medical care includes perceiving that the patient-supplier relationship fundamentally impacts close to home prosperity. At the point when medical care experts approach muscular wellbeing with sympathy, it decidedly influences the psychological and close to home versatility of people exploring these difficulties.

8. **Media Portrayal and Language Use:**

The media assumes a strong part in forming cultural discernments. Guaranteeing precise and positive portrayal of people with muscular circumstances in media can add to decreasing shame. Also, language use is significant; utilizing conscious and comprehensive language helps shift cultural mentalities.

By advancing positive stories and staying away from language that sustains generalizations, the media can effectively add to encouraging compassion in muscular wellbeing.

The brain body association in media portrayal and language use includes perceiving that the narratives and language utilized in media can impact profound prosperity. Positive and comprehensive depictions add to a more compassionate society, emphatically influencing the psychological and close to home parts of muscular wellbeing.

9. **Strong People group and Companion Compassion:**

Building strong networks is essential to lessening shame and encouraging sympathy. Peer support, where people share their encounters and sympathize with each other, makes a feeling of having a place and understanding. These people group act as places of refuge where people with muscular difficulties can track down approval, consolation, and shared insight.

The brain body association in steady networks includes perceiving that social associations and friend support contribute essentially to close to home prosperity. By cultivating sympathy inside these networks, people with muscular circumstances can explore their difficulties with a feeling of local area and understanding.

8.4 Creating Ortho-Inclusive Environments

Establishing Ortho-Comprehensive Conditions: Sustaining Openness, Compassion, and Respect

Muscular difficulties can present one of a kind obstacles for people in different parts of life, and the making of ortho-comprehensive conditions is central to guarantee openness, sympathy, and respect. This investigation digs into the significance of creating spaces, both physical and cultural, that embrace people with muscular circumstances. By cultivating inclusivity, society can add to the prosperity of those exploring muscular difficulties, perceiving the interconnected idea of physical and profound wellbeing.

1. **Grasping the Range of Muscular Difficulties:**

Muscular difficulties envelop a different range, going from constant circumstances like joint inflammation to intense wounds, medical procedures, and outer muscle problems. Understanding this range is pivotal in establishing ortho-comprehensive conditions that take care of the novel necessities of people with different muscular circumstances. From versatility constraints to the requirement for assistive gadgets, muscular difficulties can appear in changed ways, requiring smart contemplations for inclusivity.

The psyche body association in understanding the range of muscular difficulties includes perceiving that actual restrictions can affect close to home prosperity. Establishing ortho-comprehensive conditions recognizes this interconnectedness, planning to address both the apparent and undetectable parts of muscular circumstances.

2. **Actual Availability Openly Spaces:**
One of the basic components of ortho-comprehensive conditions is guaranteeing actual availability out in the open spaces. This incorporates slopes, lifts, wide entryways, and different facilities that work with simple route for people with muscular difficulties, including those utilizing versatility helps like wheelchairs or supports. By eliminating actual boundaries, society makes a comprehensive establishment that permits everybody to take part in different exercises, encouraging a feeling of having a place.

The brain body association in actual openness includes perceiving that the plan of public spaces straightforwardly influences profound prosperity. At the point when people can travel through spaces easily and without deterrent, it adds to a positive close to home insight, supporting that their presence is esteemed and obliged.

3. **Open Correspondence:**
Ortho-comprehensive conditions stretch out past actual openness to incorporate available correspondence. This includes giving data in designs that take special care of various requirements, like braille, huge print, or computerized designs. Guaranteeing that correspondence is comprehensive permits people with muscular difficulties to get to data freely, encouraging a feeling of independence and support.

The brain body association in open correspondence includes perceiving that data availability impacts profound prosperity. At the point when people can get to data without obstructions, it adds to a feeling of strengthening and decreases possible sensations of rejection, decidedly influencing their profound state.

4. **Comprehensive Working environment Practices:**
Establishing ortho-comprehensive conditions in work environments includes executing rehearses that take care of the necessities of representatives with muscular difficulties. This might incorporate giving ergonomic workstations, adaptable timetables, and facilities for people with versatility impediments. Comprehensive work environment rehearses not just help the actual prosperity

of representatives yet in addition add to a positive work culture that values variety and consideration.

The brain body association in comprehensive working environment rehearses includes perceiving that the workplace altogether impacts close to home prosperity. At the point when representatives feel upheld and obliged, it emphatically influences their psychological strength, work fulfillment, and in general profound wellbeing.

5. **Sympathy in Instructive Settings:**

Ortho-comprehensive conditions in instructive settings are fundamental for guaranteeing that understudies with muscular difficulties can completely take part in learning exercises.

This incorporates giving available study halls, assistive advances, and facilities custom-made to individual requirements. Furthermore, cultivating compassion among teachers and companions makes a strong climate where everybody can flourish scholastically and inwardly.

The brain body association in compassion inside instructive settings includes perceiving that close to home prosperity significantly impacts learning results. At the point when understudies feel comprehended, obliged, and upheld, their close to home flexibility adds to a good and improving instructive experience.

6. **Strong Medical services Practices:**

Medical care settings assume a basic part in establishing ortho-comprehensive conditions. This includes actual openness in facilities and emergency clinics as well as taking on rehearses that focus on compassionate and patient-focused care. Medical care experts who effectively pay attention to the encounters of people with muscular circumstances, address their interests, and include them in direction add to a climate that cultivates both physical and close to home prosperity.

The psyche body association in strong medical services rehearses includes perceiving that the patient-supplier relationship fundamentally impacts profound strength. At the point when medical care experts focus on compassion, it emphatically influences the psychological and profound parts of people exploring muscular difficulties.

7. **Local area Commitment and Occasions:**

Ortho-comprehensive conditions stretch out to local area commitment and occasions, guaranteeing that exercises are available to everybody. This might include choosing scenes with openness highlights, giving guest plans that oblige portability helps, and advancing occasions with comprehensive language. Making spaces where people with muscular difficulties can effectively take part in local area life cultivates a feeling of local area and having a place.

The brain body association in local area commitment includes perceiving that social collaborations add to profound prosperity. At the point when people feel remembered for local area exercises, it decidedly influences their psychological flexibility, feeling of having a place, and generally close to home wellbeing.

8. **Open Transportation:**

Transportation is a vital part of ortho-comprehensive conditions, guaranteeing that people with muscular difficulties can travel freely. This incorporates available public transportation, convenience for versatility helps, and highlights that work with simplicity of development. Available transportation upgrades actual portability as well as adds to profound prosperity by giving people the opportunity to participate in different exercises outside their homes.

The brain body association in open transportation includes perceiving that the capacity to move unreservedly locally impacts close to home strength. At the point when transportation is comprehensive, people with muscular difficulties can partake in friendly, sporting, and business related exercises, decidedly affecting their by and large profound prosperity.

9. **Support for Strategy Changes:**

Ortho-comprehensive conditions benefit from support endeavors pointed toward impacting strategy changes. Backing for comprehensive strategies that order openness guidelines in broad daylight spaces, working environments, instructive foundations, and medical care offices makes an enduring effect on cultural mentalities. By upholding for muscular inclusivity, people and associations add to a more extensive social shift that perceives and obliges the different necessities of those with muscular difficulties.

The brain body association in support for strategy changes includes perceiving that cultural designs straightforwardly impact profound prosperity. At the point when strategies reflect inclusivity, people with muscular circumstances experience a feeling of approval, acknowledgment, and pride, emphatically influencing their close to home wellbeing.

Chapter 9

Parenting Through Ortho Challenges

Nurturing Through Muscular Difficulties: Exploring the Excursion with Sympathy and Versatility

Nurturing is a compensating yet testing excursion, and when confronted with muscular difficulties inside the family, the elements can turn out to be significantly more mind boggling. Whether managing a youngster's muscular condition, injury, or the muscular soundness of a parent, the obligations and profound parts of nurturing take on extra layers. This investigation dives into the complexities of nurturing through muscular difficulties, underscoring the requirement for sympathy, flexibility, and a comprehensive methodology that tends to both the physical and close to home prosperity of the family.

1. **Grasping the Effect on Relational peculiarities:**

   Muscular difficulties inside a nuclear family can significantly affect elements. The jobs and obligations might move, and everybody in the family might have to adjust to new schedules and providing care errands.

   Understanding the effect on relational peculiarities includes perceiving the interconnected idea of these changes, with regards to down to earth changes as well as concerning profound prosperity.

   The brain body association in understanding the effect on relational peculiarities includes perceiving that profound flexibility assumes a vital part in exploring muscular difficulties. Nurturing through such circumstances requires recognizing the profound perspectives close by the actual contemplations for both the youngster and the guardians.

2. **Adjusting Providing care Liabilities:**

   Nurturing through muscular difficulties frequently includes an expanded heap of providing care liabilities. This might incorporate helping with everyday exercises, overseeing clinical arrangements, and offering profound help. Adjusting these obligations requires powerful correspondence, cooperation, and a mutual perspective inside the family.

The brain body association in adjusting providing care liabilities includes perceiving that the close to home prosperity of both the guardian and the kid is entwined with the viable parts of care. Finding some kind of harmony guarantees that the family's close to home wellbeing is sustained close by the actual consideration necessities.

3. **Engaging Youngsters and Encouraging Autonomy:**

Engaging youngsters with muscular difficulties includes encouraging a feeling of freedom while offering fundamental help. This fragile equilibrium requires grasping the kid's abilities, empowering self-articulation, and adjusting nurturing techniques to advance independence. Strengthening contributes not exclusively to the kid's actual turn of events yet additionally to their close to home prosperity.

The brain body association in enabling kids includes perceiving that a feeling of independence decidedly impacts profound versatility. Nurturing through muscular difficulties includes establishing a climate where kids feel upheld, esteemed, and able, upgrading their general prosperity.

4. **Viable Correspondence inside the Family:**

Open and viable correspondence is fundamental while nurturing through muscular difficulties. Examining feelings, concerns, and commonsense contemplations makes a strong environment where relatives feel appreciated and comprehended. Viable correspondence likewise includes age-proper conversations with kids about their muscular condition, guaranteeing straightforwardness and cultivating a feeling of trust.

The brain body association in powerful correspondence includes perceiving that close to home prosperity is profoundly impacted by the nature of family collaborations. Nurturing through muscular difficulties requires making a space where sentiments can be communicated, inquiries can be posed, and shared understanding can flourish.

5. **Adjusting Nurturing Styles:**

Nurturing styles might should be adjusted while confronting muscular difficulties inside the family. Adaptability and responsiveness become fundamental as need might arise of their kid. This versatility includes changing assumptions, putting forth sensible objectives, and offering help custom-made to the kid's muscular condition.

The brain body association in adjusting nurturing styles includes perceiving that profound prosperity is affected by the nurturing approach. A versatile and steady nurturing style adds to a positive close to home climate for both the kid and the guardians.

6. **Supporting Kin and More distant family:**

   Muscular difficulties influence the kid as well as kin and more distant family individuals. Supporting kin includes giving age-proper clarifications, tending to their interests, and encouraging a feeling of consideration. More distant family backing can be instrumental in reducing the general weight, guaranteeing that the nuclear family cooperates to give the important consideration and everyday encouragement.

   The brain body association in supporting kin and more distant family includes perceiving that profound prosperity stretches out past the singular confronting muscular difficulties. Making a steady family network decidedly impacts the close to home flexibility of all relatives.

7. **Adapting to Profound Battles:**

   Nurturing through muscular difficulties might include adapting to close to home battles, both for the youngster and the guardians. This incorporates tending to sensations of dissatisfaction, bitterness, or nervousness that might emerge. Looking for proficient daily reassurance, whether through advising or support gatherings, can be helpful in exploring these personal difficulties and encouraging versatility.

   The brain body association in adapting to close to home battles includes perceiving that profound prosperity altogether influences actual wellbeing. Focusing on psychological well-being support adds to an all encompassing methodology in nurturing through muscular difficulties.

8. **Empowering Versatile Survival strategies:**

   Empowering versatile survival strategies is fundamental for the two guardians and youngsters confronting muscular difficulties. This might include care rehearses, stress decrease methods, and developing a positive mentality. By integrating versatile survival techniques into day to day existence, the family can improve their profound strength notwithstanding muscular difficulties.

   The brain body association in empowering versatile survival techniques includes perceiving that close to home prosperity straightforwardly impacts the body's capacity to adapt to actual difficulties. Nurturing through muscular difficulties includes encouraging a strong mentality that emphatically influences both the close to home and actual parts of the family's prosperity.

9. **Observing Achievements and Accomplishments:**

Praising achievements and accomplishments, regardless of how little, turns into a significant part of nurturing through muscular difficulties. Perceiving and honoring progress adds to a positive story, imparting a feeling of achievement and lifting the general mood for both the kid and the guardians. These festivals become critical markers on the excursion of strength.

The brain body association in commending achievements includes perceiving that uplifting feedback emphatically impacts profound prosperity. Nurturing through muscular difficulties includes establishing a strong climate where accomplishments are recognized and celebrated, encouraging a deep satisfaction and inspiration.

9.1 Navigating Parental Concerns and Emotional Support

Exploring Parental Worries and Offering Close to home Help: A Comprehensive Way to deal with Family Prosperity

Nurturing is an excursion set apart by delights, challenges, and a steady obligation to the prosperity of youngsters. When confronted with muscular difficulties inside the family, parental worries might strengthen, and the requirement for basic encouragement becomes vital. This investigation digs into the complex parts of exploring parental worries and offering profound help, stressing the significance of a comprehensive methodology that includes both the physical and close to home components of family prosperity.

1. **Grasping Parental Worries Notwithstanding Muscular Difficulties:**

   Muscular difficulties inside the family summon a scope of parental worries, from the prompt stresses over the youngster's actual wellbeing to more extensive misgivings about the effect on relational peculiarities. Understanding these worries includes perceiving the interconnected idea of physical and profound prosperity. Guardians might wrestle with vulnerabilities about the future, the adequacy of medicines, and the profound strength of both the youngster and the nuclear family.

   The brain body association in understanding parental worries includes recognizing that profound prosperity essentially impacts actual wellbeing. Exploring parental worries requires a far reaching approach that tends to both the noticeable parts of muscular difficulties and the basic profound scene.

2. **All encompassing Way to deal with Muscular Difficulties:**

   Adopting an all encompassing strategy to muscular difficulties includes considering the physical, close to home, and mental components of the family's prosperity. This incorporates clinical medicines, restoration plans, and daily reassurance techniques that altogether add to the flexibility of the nuclear family. An all encompassing methodology perceives that profound prosperity isn't optional however essential to the general wellbeing of the two guardians and kids confronting muscular difficulties.

   The brain body association in a comprehensive methodology includes understanding that consistent encouragement is a fundamental part of the mending system. By tending to both the physical and close to home viewpoints, guardians can establish a climate that sustains versatility and decidedly influences the family's prosperity.

3. **Open Correspondence and Shared Direction:**

   Encouraging open correspondence inside the family is fundamental while exploring muscular difficulties. Guardians and kids ought to feel happy with talking about worries, sharing feelings, and effectively taking part in dynamic cycles connected with treatment plans. Shared dynamic enables the kid as well as makes a feeling of solidarity inside the family, permitting everybody to add to the excursion of flexibility.

   The brain body association in open correspondence includes perceiving that profound prosperity flourishes in a climate where sentiments are recognized and approved. Exploring parental worries requires making a space for open discourse, where concerns can be tended to, and choices can be made by and large.

4. **Giving Age-Suitable Data:**

   Guardians assume a significant part in giving age-suitable data to their kids about muscular difficulties. Legit conversations about the condition, treatment plans, and potential difficulties assist kids with grasping their circumstance, decreasing nervousness and cultivating a feeling of control. By fitting data to the kid's age and formative stage, guardians add to a strong climate that supports questions and self-articulation.

   The psyche body association in giving age-fitting data includes perceiving that close to home prosperity is impacted by a feeling of understanding and control. Guardians exploring muscular difficulties ought to endeavor to make an environment where kids feel educated and engaged, emphatically influencing their close to home strength.

5. **Looking for Proficient Basic encouragement:**

   Exploring parental worries frequently includes looking for proficient basic encouragement, both for guardians and the youngster. Restorative intercessions, directing administrations, or care groups can give a place of refuge to communicating feelings, tending to fears, and creating methods for dealing with especially difficult times. Proficient daily encouragement is an important asset that supplements clinical intercessions, adding to the general prosperity of the family.

   The brain body association in looking for proficient daily reassurance includes perceiving that profound flexibility is supported through restorative mediations. Guardians exploring muscular difficulties can profit from proficient direction that tends to the profound intricacies of their excursion.

6. **Empowering Profound Articulation and Approval:**

   Close to home articulation is a crucial part of exploring parental worries. Guardians ought to urge kids to communicate their feelings, whether it's apprehension, dissatisfaction, or trouble. Approval of these feelings is similarly significant, as it supports a feeling of understanding and acknowledgment. By establishing a climate where feelings are recognized and approved, guardians add to the close to home prosperity of the whole family.

The psyche body association in empowering close to home articulation includes perceiving that profound prosperity is complicatedly connected to the opportunity to communicate sentiments. Exploring parental worries requires encouraging a culture of profound transparency, permitting everybody to share their encounters and worries without judgment.

7. **Setting Sensible Assumptions and Observing Advancement:**
Setting practical assumptions is significant while exploring muscular difficulties. Guardians ought to perceive that progress might be slow and that misfortunes are a characteristic piece of the excursion. Celebrating even little achievements and recognizing the strength exhibited by the two guardians and youngsters adds to a positive story. Setting reasonable assumptions encourages a pride and inspiration inside the family.

The brain body association in setting reasonable assumptions includes perceiving that close to home prosperity is affected by the view of progress. Guardians exploring muscular difficulties ought to zero in on establishing a climate where accomplishments are recognized and celebrated, cultivating a positive profound environment.

8. **Making Routine and Steadiness:**
Muscular provokes can acquaint interruptions with day to day existence, prompting vulnerability and tension. Making routine and dependability inside the family gives a feeling of consistency and business as usual. Laying out steady schedules for feasts, exercises, and rest adds to a steady climate that upholds the close to home prosperity of the two guardians and kids.

The brain body association in making routine and solidness includes perceiving that close to home prosperity is much of the time established it might be said of safety. Exploring parental worries requires laying out a steady groundwork that permits the family to adjust to muscular difficulties while keeping a feeling of predictability.

9. **Building an Encouraging group of people:**

Building an encouraging group of people is fundamental for guardians exploring muscular difficulties. This organization might incorporate family, companions, support gatherings, or different guardians confronting comparative circumstances. Interfacing with others gives an outlet to sharing encounters, acquiring experiences, and getting basic reassurance. A solid encouraging group of people adds to the versatility of the whole family.

The psyche body association in building an encouraging group of people includes perceiving that profound prosperity is supported through friendly associations. Guardians exploring muscular difficulties ought to effectively look for and develop an encouraging group of people that comprehends and sympathizes with their excursion.

9.2 Communication Strategies with Teens

Viable Correspondence Techniques with Youngsters: Sustaining Association and Understanding

Exploring the correspondence scene with teens is a sensitive and significant part of nurturing and mentorship. Teenagers go through critical formative changes, and successful correspondence becomes fundamental for building trust, encouraging comprehension, and supporting their close to home prosperity. This investigation dives into different correspondence systems custom-made to associate with adolescents, underscoring the significance of undivided attention, compassion, and open exchange in developing positive connections.

Grasping the Teen Mentality:

Successful correspondence with youngsters starts with a significant comprehension of their interesting mentality. Puberty is a period set apart by character development, investigation, and a mission for freedom. Recognizing their requirement for independence while giving direction lays out an establishment to significant discussions. Understanding the difficulties they face, for example, peer pressure, scholarly pressure, and hormonal changes, empowers grown-ups to move toward correspondence with sympathy and persistence.

The psyche body association in understanding the young mentality includes perceiving that close to home prosperity is complicatedly attached to the difficulties and advances adolescents experience. Correspondence methodologies custom fitted to their formative stage add to a strong climate that tends to both their physical and profound necessities.

Undivided attention as a Foundation:

Undivided attention remains as a foundation in compelling correspondence with teenagers. This includes really focusing, keeping in touch, and exhibiting certifiable interest in what they need to say. Adolescents frequently value grown-ups who tune in without judgment, permitting them to offer their viewpoints, sentiments, and concerns. Undivided attention cultivates trust and signals that their viewpoints are esteemed, adding to a positive parent-youngster or guide high schooler relationship.

The brain body association in undivided attention includes perceiving that close to home prosperity thrives when people feel appreciated and comprehended. By effectively tuning in, grown-ups make a space where teenagers can share their encounters, adding to their close to home flexibility.

Sympathy as a Scaffold:

Sympathy fills in as a scaffold in correspondence with teenagers, associating grown-ups to their close to home world. Understanding and recognizing their feelings without promptly offering arrangements develops a feeling of approval. Sympathy includes imagining the youngster's perspective, perceiving the force of their sentiments, and answering with empathy. This profound association exposes the basis for and legit correspondence.

The psyche body association in sympathy includes perceiving that close to home prosperity is profoundly affected by the nature of relational associations. By communicating sympathy, grown-ups add to a positive close to home climate, cultivating trust and understanding.

Open and Non-Critical Exchange:

Encouraging open and non-critical exchange is crucial while speaking with youngsters. Establishing a climate where they feel happy with sharing their considerations and encounters empowers transparency. Keeping away from prompt judgment, analysis, or cavalier responses permits youngsters to legitimately communicate their thoughts. The objective is to lay out a space where they have a real sense of security examining both positive and testing parts of their lives.

The psyche body association in open and non-critical exchange includes perceiving that close to home prosperity flourishes in a climate liberated from dread of judgment. By advancing open correspondence, grown-ups add to the profound strength of teenagers, giving a stage to them to explore their encounters.

Regarding Their Points of view:

Regarding adolescents' viewpoints is vital in successful correspondence. While grown-ups may offer direction in light of involvement, recognizing and regarding the teenagers' perspectives cultivates a feeling of organization.

In any event, when viewpoints vary, moving toward discussions with shared regard upgrades the nature of correspondence. It flags that their viewpoints are esteemed, adding to a positive and cooperative dynamic.

The psyche body association in regarding points of view includes perceiving that profound prosperity is impacted by a feeling of independence and approval. By regarding teenagers' perspectives, grown-ups add to their profound strength, enabling them to explore difficulties with certainty.

Laying out Clear Limits:

Powerful correspondence with youngsters includes laying out clear and sensible limits. While independence is significant, laying out rules assists teenagers with figuring out assumptions and results. Clear limits give a feeling that everything is good and construction, adding to a sound correspondence dynamic. Grown-ups can include teenagers in conversations about rules and results, cultivating a cooperative methodology that energizes liability.

The brain body association in laying out clear limits includes perceiving that close to home prosperity is entwined with a feeling of safety. By defining clear limits, grown-ups add to a stable profound climate for youngsters, advancing a harmony among freedom and direction.

Using Innovation Mindfully:

In the computerized age, it is unavoidable to integrate innovation into correspondence. Grown-ups can embrace innovation as a device for association, remaining informed about teenagers' web-based exercises, and taking part in computerized spaces. In any case, dependable innovation use includes defining limits, examining on the web wellbeing, and advancing solid screen time propensities. Using innovation mindfully cultivates a feeling of trust while guaranteeing a decent way to deal with correspondence.

The psyche body association in using innovation mindfully includes perceiving that profound prosperity is impacted by the nature of online connections. By exploring innovation use dependably, grown-ups add to a positive computerized climate, cultivating a good arrangement among virtual and eye to eye correspondence.

Empowering Freedom and Direction:

Empowering freedom and dynamic engages teenagers in their correspondence with grown-ups. Permitting them to simply decide, assume liability, and gain from their choices constructs certainty. While direction stays pivotal, working with open doors for adolescents to practice independence adds to their profound versatility. This approach signals trust in their capacities and urges a proactive way to deal with correspondence.

The psyche body association in empowering freedom includes perceiving that profound prosperity flourishes when people feel a feeling of organization and self-viability. By empowering freedom, grown-ups add to the close to home strength of teenagers, cultivating a mentality of obligation and responsibility.

Developing a Positive Climate:

Establishing a positive climate is basic to successful correspondence with youngsters. A family or mentorship setting portrayed by inspiration, backing, and support upgrades the nature of cooperations. Recognizing accomplishments, communicating appreciation, and encouraging a feeling of having a place add to a good close to home air, working with open correspondence.

The brain body association in developing a positive climate includes perceiving that profound prosperity is impacted by the general air of the family or mentorship setting. By developing energy, grown-ups add to the profound versatility of teenagers, making a space where they feel upheld and esteemed.

9.3 Empowering Parents to Address Ortho Hurdles

Engaging Guardians to Address Muscular Obstacles: A Far reaching Way to deal with Family Prosperity

Nurturing through muscular difficulties requires versatility, flexibility, and an exhaustive comprehension of both the physical and profound parts of the excursion. At the point when a kid faces muscular obstacles, guardians become focal figures in offering help, exploring medicines, and encouraging a climate that supports the general prosperity of the family. This investigation dives into engaging guardians to address muscular obstacles, stressing a comprehensive methodology that envelops actual consideration, everyday encouragement, and the development of versatility.

1. **Grasping the Effect of Muscular Obstacles on Families:**
   Engaging guardians to address muscular obstacles starts with a profound comprehension of the effect such difficulties can have on families. Muscular circumstances or wounds might disturb everyday schedules, present vulnerabilities about the future, and require changes in nurturing styles. Perceiving the profound cost for both the kid and the nuclear family permits guardians to move toward the circumstance with compassion and a proactive outlook.
   The psyche body association in understanding the effect includes perceiving that profound prosperity is unpredictably connected to how families explore and adjust to muscular obstacles. A far reaching approach recognizes the interconnectedness of physical and profound wellbeing inside the relational intricacy.

2. **Giving Instruction and Data:**
   Engaging guardians begins with giving complete instruction and data about the particular muscular difficulties their youngster is confronting. This includes straightforward correspondence with medical care experts, grasping therapy choices, and acquiring bits of knowledge into expected long haul impacts. Equipped with information, guardians can effectively take part in direction, pose informed inquiries, and give their kid age-proper data about their condition.
   The brain body association in giving schooling includes perceiving that profound prosperity is much of the time affected by the degree of understanding and control guardians feel in regards to their youngster's muscular obstacles. Admittance to data empowers guardians to explore the excursion with certainty, decidedly affecting both their close to home strength and that of their youngster.

3. **Exploring Profound Reactions:**
   Muscular obstacles frequently inspire a scope of close to home reactions from guardians, including stress, nervousness, and once in a while responsibility. Enabling guardians includes recognizing and exploring these close to home reactions in a sound way. Making a space for open correspondence inside the family, looking for basic reassurance when required, and understanding that it's generally expected to encounter a scope of feelings add to close to home strength.
   The psyche body association in exploring close to home reactions includes perceiving that profound prosperity is profoundly entwined with the capacity to communicate and handle feelings. By tending to close to home reactions transparently, guardians establish a climate that encourages versatility and flexibility.

4. **Adjusting Providing care Liabilities:**
   Muscular difficulties frequently accompany expanded providing care liabilities. Enabling guardians to adjust these obligations includes laying out clear correspondence and joint effort inside the family. Circulating undertakings, looking for outside help when required, and cultivating collaboration add to a decent providing care approach. This guarantees that guardians can meet the actual necessities of their youngster while keeping up with their own prosperity.

The brain body association in adjusting providing care liabilities includes perceiving that profound prosperity is intently attached to how guardians oversee pressure and responsibility. By accomplishing an equilibrium in providing care liabilities, guardians add to their own close to home versatility and establish a steady climate for their youngster.

5. **Empowering Versatile Survival techniques:**

Engaging guardians incorporates empowering the improvement of versatile survival techniques for both themselves and their youngster. This includes distinguishing sound ways of adapting to pressure, vulnerability, and difficulties. Displaying successful survival techniques and cultivating a mentality of flexibility add to a positive close to home climate inside the family.

The brain body association in empowering versatile survival techniques includes perceiving that profound prosperity is impacted by the capacity to adapt to difficulties in a helpful way. By integrating versatile methods for dealing with especially difficult times, guardians add to a strong relational peculiarity.

6. **Advancing a Positive Nurturing Climate:**

Establishing a positive nurturing climate is fundamental while tending to muscular obstacles. This includes praising accomplishments, encouraging a feeling of business as usual, and advancing an inspirational perspective. Perceiving and supporting the qualities of both the youngster and the family add to a sustaining climate that upgrades close to home prosperity.

The psyche body association in advancing a positive nurturing climate includes perceiving that profound prosperity is intently attached to the general air inside the family. By advancing energy, guardians make a space where their kid can flourish inwardly, encouraging a feeling that everything is good and prosperity.

7. **Building an Encouraging group of people:**

Enabling guardians to address muscular obstacles incorporates building a powerful encouraging group of people. This organization might incorporate medical services experts, support gatherings, companions, and relatives. Interfacing with other people who have encountered comparative difficulties gives a feeling of local area, understanding, and shared information.

The brain body association in building an encouraging group of people includes perceiving that profound prosperity is supported through friendly associations. By building an encouraging group of people, guardians make roads for everyday reassurance, direction, and shared encounters, adding to their versatility.

8. **Encouraging Freedom in the Youngster:**

Engaging guardians includes cultivating freedom in their youngster, in any event, while confronting muscular difficulties. Empowering age-suitable independence, including the youngster in navigation, and advancing a mentality of self-viability add to their profound prosperity. Perceiving and praising the kid's capacities and achievements encourage a deep satisfaction and freedom.

The psyche body association in cultivating freedom includes perceiving that profound prosperity is firmly connected to a feeling of organization and achievement. By encouraging autonomy, guardians add to the close to home versatility and confidence of their youngster.

9. **Looking for Proficient Daily reassurance:**

Recognizing the profound cost of muscular obstacles, guardians ought to feel enabled to look for proficient daily encouragement when required. This might include guiding, treatment, or joining guardian support gatherings. Proficient everyday reassurance gives a place of refuge to guardians to communicate their sentiments, gain survival methods, and explore the close to home intricacies of the excursion.

The brain body association in looking for proficient everyday encouragement includes perceiving that close to home prosperity is supported through remedial mediations. By getting to proficient help, guardians add to their own profound flexibility and make an establishment for a strong family climate.

9.4 Family Dynamics and Ortho Wellness

Relational intricacies and Muscular Health: Sustaining Backing and Flexibility

Relational peculiarities assume a vital part in molding the prosperity of people confronting muscular difficulties. At the point when a relative, especially a kid, experiences muscular obstacles, the elements inside the nuclear family go through changes that stretch out past the actual parts of care. This investigation dives into the unpredictable exchange between relational peculiarities and muscular wellbeing, stressing the significance of a steady climate, compelling correspondence, and the development of strength inside the family.

1. **The Effect of Muscular Health on Relational peculiarities:**
   Muscular wellbeing, or the difficulties related with muscular circumstances, fundamentally impacts relational intricacies. The presentation of clinical medicines, rehabilitative cycles, and potential way of life changes can reshape the jobs and obligations of relatives. Understanding the effect includes perceiving the requirement for transformation, adaptability, and open correspondence to encourage a climate helpful for muscular health.

   The brain body association in the effect of muscular health includes recognizing that profound prosperity is unpredictably connected to the family's capacity to explore and adjust to these difficulties. A family's reaction to muscular obstacles can fundamentally impact the close to home versatility and generally prosperity of every part.

2. **Steady Climate as an Establishment:**
   Laying out a strong climate fills in as the establishment for cultivating muscular wellbeing inside the family. This includes making a space where every relative feels appreciated, esteemed, and comprehended.

A steady climate recognizes the one of a kind requirements of the singular confronting muscular difficulties, advancing a feeling of safety and trust that is pivotal for both physical and profound prosperity.

The psyche body association in a steady climate includes perceiving that close to home prosperity flourishes in an air of understanding and consolation. By focusing on help, families add to the close to home flexibility of people exploring muscular obstacles, cultivating a positive and durable dynamic.

3. **Compelling Correspondence and Straightforwardness:**

   Compelling correspondence is principal in tending to muscular wellbeing inside the family. Straightforward conversations about the condition, treatment plans, and potential difficulties make a common perspective. It permits relatives to communicate their interests, seek clarification on some pressing issues, and effectively take part in direction, encouraging a cooperative methodology that improves profound prosperity.

   The psyche body association in powerful correspondence includes perceiving that profound prosperity is profoundly impacted by the nature of family collaborations. By advancing open and straightforward correspondence, families add to a positive profound climate that upholds muscular health.

4. **Adjusting Jobs and Obligations:**

   Muscular difficulties frequently require a change in jobs and obligations inside the family. Adjusting to new providing care assignments, obliging clinical arrangements, and offering close to home help become indispensable parts. Families that explore these transformations with adaptability and common comprehension add to a climate where muscular wellbeing isn't just tended to genuinely yet additionally inwardly.

   The psyche body association in adjusting jobs and obligations includes perceiving that profound prosperity is entwined with how families appropriate and oversee providing care assignments. By cultivating versatility, families add to the profound flexibility of both the person with muscular difficulties and other relatives.

5. **Encouraging Versatility and Survival methods:**

   The excursion through muscular obstacles requires flexibility and survival methods inside the family. This includes recognizing difficulties, praising achievements, and developing a mentality that embraces the two difficulties and triumphs. Families that cultivate strength establish a strong climate that supports the improvement of versatile ways of dealing with especially difficult times, decidedly influencing the close to home prosperity, everything being equal.

   The brain body association in encouraging strength includes perceiving that close to home prosperity is profoundly associated with the family's capacity to explore difficulties with an uplifting perspective. By imparting flexibility, families add to the close to home strength expected to face muscular obstacles earnestly and good faith.

6. **Encouraging groups of people and Local area Commitment:**
Drawing in with encouraging groups of people and the local area assumes a critical part in upgrading muscular wellbeing inside the family. Interfacing with different families confronting comparable difficulties, partaking in help gatherings, and drawing in with medical care experts make an organization that gives important bits of knowledge, consistent reassurance, and a feeling of having a place. The feeling of local area decidedly influences the close to home versatility of families exploring muscular obstacles.

The psyche body association in encouraging groups of people includes perceiving that close to home prosperity is sustained through friendly associations. By effectively captivating with encouraging groups of people, families add to the close to home versatility of every part, cultivating a feeling of shared encounters and understanding.

7. **Observing Advancement and Accomplishments:**
Celebrating progress, regardless of how little, turns into a fundamental part of muscular wellbeing inside the family. Recognizing accomplishments, whether they are connected with actual achievements or close to home versatility, adds to a positive story. Families that celebrate progress establish a climate where every part feels esteemed and upheld, emphatically affecting their close to home prosperity.

The brain body association in celebrating progress includes perceiving that profound prosperity is affected by the view of accomplishment and affirmation. By praising achievements, families add to the close to home versatility of people confronting muscular difficulties, cultivating a deep satisfaction and inspiration.

8. **Empowering Freedom and Independence:**

Muscular health inside the family includes empowering freedom and independence for the singular confronting difficulties. This might incorporate advancing taking care of oneself, including the person in navigation, and cultivating a feeling of organization. Families that urge freedom add to the close to home prosperity of the individual, permitting them to explore their difficulties with a feeling of control and self-viability.

The brain body association in empowering freedom includes perceiving that profound prosperity is firmly connected to a feeling of independence and self-assurance. By cultivating freedom, families add to the close to home flexibility of people confronting muscular obstacles, advancing a positive and enabling dynamic.